The

Reference

Shelf

U.S. Foreign Policy Since the Cold War

Edited by Richard Joseph Stein

The Reference Shelf
Volume 73 • Number 4

The H.W. Wilson Company
2001

The Reference Shelf

The books in this series contain reprints of articles, excerpts from books, addresses on current issues, and studies of social trends in the United States and other countries. There are six separately bound numbers in each volume, all of which are usually published in the same calendar year. Numbers one through five are each devoted to a single subject, providing background information and discussion from various points of view and concluding with a subject index and comprehensive bibliography that lists books, pamphlets, and abstracts of additional articles on the subject. The final number of each volume is a collection of recent speeches, and it contains a cumulative speaker index. Books in the series may be purchased individually or on subscription.

Library of Congress has cataloged this serial title as follows:

U.S. foreign policy since the Cold War / edited by Richard Joseph Stein.
    p.cm.—(The reference shelf; v. 73, no. 4)
  Includes bibliographical references and index.
  ISBN 0-8242-0993-1
  1. United States—Foreign relations—1989– I. Stein, Richard Joseph. II. Series.

E840 .U1718 2001

2001035983

Visit H.W. Wilson's Web site: www.hwwilson.com

Printed in the United States of America

Contents

Preface

The end of World War II replaced the old system of European "great powers" with two superpowers: the United States and the Soviet Union. As a devastated Europe began reconstruction, the superpowers engaged in a conflict of ideology between the communist system of the Soviets and the capitalist system of the United States. The conflict would be known as the "Cold War" and last for forty years, involving ten U.S. presidents and two major military operations, in Korea and Vietnam.

Nuclear apocalypse was the primary fear during the Cold War. This threat climaxed with the Cuban Missile Crisis in 1962, when Soviet leader Nikita Khrushchev built missile launching sites in Cuba aimed at the United States. Fear of nuclear Armageddon inspired the Anti-Ballistic Missile Treaty of 1972, which limited the number of warheads for each country, "proceeding from the premise that nuclear war would have devastating consequences for all mankind," as the original documents stated. The United States practiced containment as a strategy for preventing the expansion of a hostile power or ideology without engaging in outright war.

The Cold War continued as a mind game through the 1980s between Soviet leader Gorbachev and U.S. President Ronald Reagan, who called the Soviet Union "an evil empire." Reagan even planned an unexecuted missile defense system known as "Star Wars" to deflect Soviet ballistic missiles. Nonetheless, there was little direct confrontation between the two countries up to the collapse of the Soviet Union in 1991; instead, the Cold War between the superpowers was enacted by proxy, in such regions as Afghanistan and Nicaragua.

With Russia now a struggling democracy, the United States has become the most powerful nation in the world, with new and more scattered conflicts facing the nation. European nations are collaborating to create a European Union that may eventually equal the United States in power. Countries hostile to the U.S.—North Korea, Iraq, and China—either have nuclear weapons or threaten to develop them. Supporters of international extremist groups have the resources to perpetrate acts of terrorism on American soil.

In the last decade, the United States has engaged in world affairs more overtly than during the Cold War. The nation's traditional policy of isolationism has changed to a foreign policy of intervention in virtually all corners of the world. The post–Cold War era began with a U.S.-led, multinational military operation against Iraq when that country invaded Kuwait. The month-long war, punctuated by the use of U.S. "smart bombs," demonstrated the U.S. military superiority that continues today.

Attempts by the U.S. to influence global politics have caused tension between America and its allies in Europe and Russia, who have protested against a number of U.S. policies and fear American hegemony in military affairs. Meanwhile, relations with China, now the most powerful communist nation on earth, remain one of the most serious post–Cold War foreign policy challenges for the U.S., especially in light of China's dubious human rights record and its influence on South Asian politics.

U.S. foreign policy has long involved attempts to disseminate democracy and capitalism throughout the world, and the end of the Cold War has given the nation unique leverage to do so. *U.S. Foreign Policy Since the Cold War* includes several articles that address this issue particularly, but this is only one of the many foreign policy challenges that have emerged in the last 10 years. The first section of the book, "America's Approach to Foreign Policy," provides a general sense of American international relations in theory and practice, including an article from Ambassador John W. McDonald on American diplomatic style. The second section, "European Relations," presents views of the U.S. from our strongest allies. This section shows that America is not always seen by the outside world as a grand protector of democracy and social justice. "Military Intervention," the third section, examines America's involvement in Middle East confrontations, the costs of maintaining an advanced military, and views of a missile defense system. The fourth section, "China and 'Rogue States,'" looks at the tense U.S. relationships with Cuba, North Korea, and Vietnam—all considered "rogue states" because of their unpredictable and aggressive regimes and their apparent disregard for international law—and the almost equally difficult relationship with China. The articles in the fifth section, "Terrorism," speculate on the rise of international terrorism and its use as a form of warfare between countries. The section also addresses terrorist actions within the United States and includes an excerpt from a speech by the former head of the F.B.I., Louis Freeh. The final section, "Spies Like Us . . . and Them," considers a Cold War remnant that persists into the post–Cold War era. Articles in this section look at the espionage activities of the C.I.A. and the now defunct K.G.B.; the case of former F.B.I. agent and Russian spy Robert Hanssen; the politics of getting caught; the importance of continuing to spy on China; and a museum dedicated to the Cold War.

The editor wishes to thank the individuals in the General Reference department at the H.W. Wilson Company for their assistance: Lynn Messina, Norris Smith, Sandra Watson, Jennifer Peloso, Gray Young, Jacquelene Latif, and Tia Brown. I am grateful for their contributions, insights, and support.

Richard Joseph Stein
August 2001

Timeline of U.S. Foreign Policy
Since the Cold War

1991

- Iraq invades Kuwait, causing the United States to lead a United Nations coalition to force Iraq out of the country in the Persian Gulf War.
- The U.S. and Soviet Union sign a Strategic Arms Reduction Talks (START) treaty pledging a 30 percent reduction in nuclear weapons.
- The Soviet Union dissolves and Mikhail Gorbachev resigns, yielding power to Boris Yeltsin, the first elected leader of Russia.

1992

- The U.N. sends peacekeeping troops to the Balkans when the Yugoslavian government resists attempts by Slovenia and Croatia to secede. The European Community and the U.S. formally recognize Bosnia-Herzegovina, Slovenia, and Croatia as independent countries.
- The European Community (now European Union) ratifies the Maastrict treaty, which not only creates a common currency (euro), but also moves to build a unified foreign policy among its member nations.
- The U.S. returns the Subic Bay Naval Base to the Philippine government.
- A U.S.-led multinational force enters war-torn Somalia as U.N. peacekeepers.

1993

- Bill Clinton is sworn in as U.S. president.
- The U.S. and Russia create a new START treaty to further cuts in their nuclear arsenals.
- The U.S. ratifies the North American Free Trade Agreement (NAFTA) between Canada, the U.S., and Mexico.
- Six people die in the terrorist bombing of the World Trade Center in New York.
- Israel and the Palestinian Liberation Organization sign a peace agreement brokered by the U.S.
- North Korea withdraws from the Nuclear Non-Proliferation Treaty.
- The U.S. airdrops supplies to persecuted Bosnian Muslims in the former Yugoslavia.

1994

- The U.S. renews trade with China and Vietnam.
- North Korea rejects U.S. and U.N. inspection of its nuclear facilities.
- The U.S. and Cuba agree on emigration laws applying to Cuban refugees fleeing to Florida.
- Haiti permits occupation by U.S. troops as its military regime is overthrown and the democratically elected Jean-Bertrand Aristide is returned to power.
- The U.S military oversees the evacuation of U.N. peacekeepers in Somalia after the U.S. and Europe suffer several casualties and the U.N. fails to resolve conflicts among the nation's clans.

1995

- The U.S. Congress asks for increased defense spending and a reduction in U.N. efforts. President Clinton vetoes the proposed measures.
- NATO launches air strikes against Serbia.
- Leaders of Bosnia, Croatia, and Serbia meet in Dayton, OH, for peace talks and agree upon a cease-fire.
- The U.S. gives Mexico $10 billion in loans for its failed economy.

1996

- The U.S. Navy frees foreign nationals in Liberia.
- START II is signed by the U.S. and Russia.
- The U.S. peacekeeping mission in Haiti is taken over by the U.N.
- The U.S. attacks Iraq after the latter country intervenes in Kurdish territory.

1997

- NATO stops a coup attempt by Bosnian police against the Bosnian government.
- The Czech Republic, Hungary, and Poland join NATO.
- START III is signed by Boris Yeltsin and Bill Clinton.
- U.S. economic sanctions against Cuba cause protest by European leaders, and the World Trade Organization threatens intervention.
- Zaire becomes the Republic of the Congo and is recognized by the U.S. government.

1998

- President Clinton denounces past U.S. support for African dictatorships.

- The U.S. mediates a peace settlement in Northern Ireland.

- Pope John Paul II visits Cuba, denouncing the Castro-led communist government and U.S. sanctions against the country.

- President Clinton visits Beijing to strengthen economic ties with China.

- Palestinian and Israeli leaders meet in the U.S. to negotiate Palestinian statehood.

- The U.S. House of Representatives votes to impeach the president for committing perjury in his testimony concerning White House sex scandals. The Senate votes against impeachment, and the President remains in office.

- U.S. embassies are bombed in Kenya and Tanzania. The U.S. military retaliates by bombing terrorist bases in the Sudan and Afghanistan.

- Reluctantly, Iraq lets the U.N. inspect its nuclear arsenal. The U.S. bombs Iraqi facilities, including military and intelligence bases, after Iraqi leader Saddam Hussein tries to block the inspection.

1999

- The U.S. and U.N. leave Haiti.

- China enters the World Trade Organization with the support of President Clinton.

- The Chinese government is accused of spying on American nuclear weapons facilities.

- NATO bombs Serbian military targets. Yuoglavian leader Slobodan Milosevic's ethnic cleansing tactics expel over one million Albanians from Kosovo.

- Protests erupt during the World Trade Organization meeting in Seattle, WA.

- The Comprehensive Test Ban Treaty, signed by President Clinton and other world leaders, is rejected by the U.S. Senate.

2000

- The World Bank and the International Monetary Fund call for reform at a meeting in Washington, D.C.

- The U.S. gives one billion dollars to the Colombian government to stop illegal drug exports.

- The U.S. Congress votes for trade relations with the Chinese government.
- START II and the Comprehensive Test Ban Treaty are threatened by the American antiballistic missile system.
- Elián González, the young Cuban refugee who fled to Florida with his mother in November 1999, is returned to his father in Cuba by order of the U.S. courts.
- Vladimir Putin becomes Russian president, while George W. Bush is elected U.S. president.

2001

- The nuclear submarine U.S.S. *Greenville* accidentally strikes and sinks a Japanese fishing boat off the coast of Hawaii, killing nine people.
- Longtime F.B.I. agent Robert Philip Hanssen is arrested and charged with spying for the K.G.B. He pleads guilty to avoid the death penalty.
- President Bush provokes vehement protests abroad when he announces that the U.S. would not require utility companies to control carbon dioxide emissions, effectively removing the U.S. from the Kyoto Protocol, an international attempt to slow the pace of global warming.
- A U.S. Navy spy plane collides with a Chinese fighter off the southern coast of China and makes an emergency landing on Hainan Island, where the Chinese government detains both the crew and the plane. The crew are released 12 days later, but the plane, with its intelligence gear, is held by the Chinese for several months.
- The Bush administration begins talks with Mexico about increasing the numbers and altering the status of guest workers.
- At a summit meeting in Quebec, President Bush advocates a Free Trade Area of the Americas but suggests that it be limited to democracies.
- Affirming an arms deal with Taiwan in the face of formal protests from China, President Bush says the U.S. would do "whatever it took" to defend the island.
- The Bush administration announces its intent to build a missile defense shield and cut America's nuclear arsenal, placing the emphasis on defense rather than retaliation.
- President Bush travels to Europe to meet with Russian president Vladimir Putin and European heads of state, to explain U.S. positions on global warming and missile defense.

Sources: Steven W. Hook and John Spanier, *American Foreign Policy Since World War II*, CQ Press (Washington, D.C., 2000); and Joseph Nathan Kane, Janet Podell, and Steven Anzovin, *Facts About the Presidents*, 8th ed., H.W. Wilson Company (New York, 2001).

I. America's Approach to Foreign Policy

Lionel Cironneau/AP Photo

East German guards watch as demonstrators tear down a section of the Berlin Wall on November 9, 1989. While this moment marked the symbolic end of the Cold War, it would take two more years for the Soviet Union to dissolve and for the Cold War to be officially over.

Editor's Introduction

Emerging as a superpower in the years after World War II, the United States engaged in a long Cold War struggle against the Soviet Union, its principal rival for global domination. Both nations formed strategic alliances with smaller countries, conducting wars by proxy and using covert subversion while amassing formidable nuclear arsenals. The obvious dangers posed by such weapons, however, prompted the rivals to shrink from full-scale military confrontation, conducting a war of nerves until the political and economic collapse of the Soviet Union in 1991 left the United States the most powerful country in the world. But instead of one great rival, the United States now had to contend with numerous smaller unfriendly regimes, an emergent superpower (China), trans-national terrorist organizations, and a global landscape with potentially explosive trouble spots, particularly in the Balkans and the Middle East. A different sort of foreign policy would be needed, to address a different set of problems and successfully protect America's national interests in a rapidly changing environment. The nation's long-term commitment to promoting democracy, human rights, and free trade around the world might also be tested.

The first two articles in this section present overviews of U.S. foreign relations in theory and practice. Ambassador John W. McDonald gives his perspective on American diplomacy since the nation's emergence as the lone superpower in "An American's View of the U.S. Negotiating Style." He defines U.S. diplomatic strengths, such as the abilities to be friendly and fair, and lists its faults, such as arrogance and impatience. In "U.S. 'Global Leadership': A Euphemism for World Policeman," Barbara Conry of the Cato Institute examines American political and military intervention abroad and argues that the U.S. should not be the world's chief international law enforcer. She discusses America's role as global leader and explains the costs of intervention, both financial and emotional.

The inauguration of a new U.S. president is always accompanied by a great deal of speculation and some trepidation, both among American politicos and among government leaders abroad, and the changing of the guard that occurred in 2001 has been no exception. "The 900-Pound Gorilla" from *Newsday* examines George W. Bush's foreign policy approach as he takes office in a time when America is experiencing a period of enormous prosperity and relative peace. This article includes arguments for and against Bush's proposed National Missile Defense system and speculation about America's future role in chronically troubled regions, such as the Middle East. In the next piece,

"Bush Aides Cite 'Realism' In Tougher Foreign Policy," Bob Deans reports on the president's hard-nosed attitude towards former Cold War adversaries, including Russia, North Korea, and China, the latter increasingly viewed as an emerging threat to global stability. Finally, Peter Hakim of the *Christian Science Monitor* suggests five ways America can develop better relations with South American nations, including a free trade agreement that is more favorable to both parties.

An American's View of the U.S. Negotiating Style[1]

By Ambassador John W. McDonald
American Diplomacy, February 5, 2001

After reviewing my own experience of forty years as an American diplomat and international negotiator, I have developed my own personal definition of a U.S. negotiating style. This definition bears in mind that any style of negotiation is tempered and influenced by the personality and the ability of the individual negotiator, as well as the cultural, political, emotional, and physical situations surrounding the negotiations. In fact, the cases in this issue suggest strongly that many factors, in addition to style, are at work in shaping the process and outcome of international negotiations, including tactics strategy, the structure of the negotiations, and external influences, to name a few.

I believe the following characteristics, both positive and negative, taken collectively, define a U.S. negotiating style.

Impatient—We are the most impatient people in the world. This characteristic is carried over into our negotiating style to such an extent that the rest of the world recognizes this trait in our negotiators and takes advantage of it at every opportunity. Impatience is such an ingrained, subconscious tendency in most Americans that they don't even realize the rest of the world marches to the tune of a different drummer. Different perceptions of time cause many misunderstandings during negotiations.

Arrogant—Most other peoples believe that we are the most arrogant, or certainly one of the most arrogant, nations in the world. Our superpower is certainly a part of this image. This power-based arrogance is often projected by our negotiators across the conference table at international gatherings. Often such arrogance is seen by others as our second nature. We seem to project the belief that we are superior to other peoples because we have led the world for fifty years and know that we are best in everything we do. Many Americans are actually surprised when they are accused by non-Americans of possessing this characteristic and frequently take exception to this criticism, thereby making matters worse.

Listening—We are not good listeners. This goes hand in hand with impatience and arrogance. Because we have not developed good listening skills, which require patience, we are assumed to be superficial and uninterested in other points of view, and therefore arrogant.

Insular—Most Americans have limited experience with regard to other cultures. This shortcoming can often lead to mistakes, misunderstandings and subsequent embarrassment on the part of the

---

Because our law schools teach students to go out and win, we are trained in the win-lose concept of negotiations: I win—you lose.

Americans. Such restricted experience often leads to a feeling of insecurity on the part of the Americans and may result in their making a limited outreach towards other delegates. Rarely is this misinterpreted by others as shyness, but rather as a lack of interest. It may also be considered to be part of an American superiority complex.

Legalistic—The majority of American negotiators are lawyers. This means that they are intelligent, hardworking, adversarial, usually dedicated to the task at hand, and legalistic. Legalistic, in this context, means concerned with detail. We are less interested in general principles, or with the larger picture, and are more interested in the fine print of the agreement. It also means that when an agreement is reached, we consider it final. It is not subject to being reopened or renegotiated. Because our law schools teach students to go out and win, we are trained in the win-lose concept of negotiations: I win—you lose. International negotiations today are more and more frequently based on a consensus building approach or win-win philosophy

Naive—Our insular attitude, and sometimes our appearance, can give the impression that we are naive, are easy marks for the skilled negotiator and are someone to be taken advantage of. This can actually happen to a newcomer to the international negotiating arena, but the impression is usually incorrect and not long lasting. In fact, the characteristics of naivete, can be turned around, to the advantage of the American negotiator.

Friendly—We are recognized as being friendly, out-going, and having a sense of humor. This trait is particularly important. Being friendly helps to build a sense of trust among negotiators. Having a sense of humor, at the right time, is essential because it can be used to break tension and often helps to move a difficult negotiating process along, towards a satisfactory conclusion.

Fair—We are perceived as believing in fair play and honesty. This characteristic is widely recognized throughout the international community, and respected.

Flexible—U.S. negotiators have more authority to make decisions during negotiations than most other delegations. This means that they can often make decisions on the spot, at the conference table. This flexibility is due to the fact that [a] good negotiator is trusted by his headquarters. He has also built some negotiating flexibility into the U.S. position, before leaving for the conference. In addition, U.S. delegations are larger than most other delegations because they include subject matter experts, who often have the answers to substantive questions at their fingertips. This enables the United States to project a positive image and to adapt the U.S. position more quickly and more easily than other delegations in order to meet a new situation or a particular issue that has just arisen.

Risk Takers—More so than most, U.S. negotiators are risk takers. They are often prepared to put forward new and innovative ideas, suggestions for compromise, even specific language that can move the conference towards agreement. This is often done without prior approval from headquarters and represents the risk the head of delegation is prepared to take, in order to reach consensus. This trait is widely recognized and highly respected by other delegations.

Pragmatic—The U.S. point of view is usually a practical, pragmatic one. We are rarely interested in high-flown rhetoric, long, flowery speeches or a dogmatic, ideological point of view. We want to get on with discussing the substance of the issues on the agenda and try to reach some practical conclusion about the matter at hand.

Preparation—We are usually the best prepared delegation at the conference table. We go to extraordinary lengths, often starting many months in advance of a conference, to prepare position papers, briefing books, and background documentation. The U.S. delegation attempts to anticipate every issue that might arise during the negotiations and develop a response to that situation, ready to be used at the conference. All position papers prepared for intergovernmental negotiations are approved in advance by each agency in the executive branch that has an interest in that subject. This is time and effort well spent and is reflected repeatedly in the final positive results of the negotiations.

Cooperative—Americans are cooperative. They are aware of the importance of interagency coordination in the development of U.S. positions papers. At the conference itself they recognize the necessity for working and cooperating with other delegations, the conference secretariat, the press, nongovernmental organization representatives, and the private business sector. They also recognize the authority of the head of their delegation and acknowledge the importance of the delegation's need to speak with one voice on an issue.

I believe that a combination of these characteristics can be found in all of the American delegates who represent the United States Government at the one thousand annual, international, intergovernmental conferences the United States attends. There may be other traits which could be added to the list of attributes defining a U.S. negotiating style. It is clear, however, that the positive characteristics outweigh the negative ones. With awareness, training, skill, and study, the negative traits can be changed and corrected. When this is achieved, our negotiators will be more effective and be viewed by the rest of the world with even greater esteem and respect.

U.S. "Global Leadership"

A Euphemism for World Policeman[2]

BY BARBARA CONRY
CATO INSTITUTE, FEBRUARY 5, 1997

Introduction: From Containment to Leadership

The U.S. foreign policy community has been grasping for a national security strategy since the end of the Cold War nullified the doctrine of containment. From former president George Bush's proclamation of the "new world order" to the Clinton administration's strategies of "enlargement" and "assertive multilateralism," Washington has found containment a tough act to follow. Gradually, though, a bumper-sticker approach to foreign policy has emerged upon which almost everyone can agree: U.S. "leadership" in world affairs.

Pundits of varying ideological persuasions and high-level policy-makers from both parties have embraced the notion of global leadership as a guiding principle of U.S. foreign policy. Former secretary of state Warren Christopher has written, "America must lead. . . . American leadership is our first principle and a central lesson of this century. The simple fact is that if we do not lead, no one else will."[1] Republican presidential nominee Bob Dole echoed Christopher's sentiments, declaring, "Only the United States can lead on the full range of political, diplomatic, economic, and military issues confronting the world."[2] House Speaker Newt Gingrich has joined the chorus:

> We have to lead the world. . . . If we don't lead the world I think that we have a continuing decay into anarchy, I think we have more and more violence around the planet, and I think it is highly unlikely anybody will replace us in leadership roles in the next 30 years.[3]

Christopher, Dole, and Gingrich have at times had serious disagreements about the conduct of foreign policy. Their agreement on the need for U.S. global leadership does not indicate consensus but instead reflects the ambiguity of global leadership as a basis for

---

2. Article by Barbara Conry from *Cato Institute* February 5, 1997. Copyright © *Cato Institute*. Reprinted with permission.

U.S. strategy. Anyone can invoke the mantra of U.S. global leadership because its meaning is in the mind of the speaker. As Jessica Mathews of the Council on Foreign Relations has pointed out, "Rhetorically, at least, nearly everyone agrees on the undiminished need for American leadership. But the word is used to mask profoundly different views of America's role in the world."[4]

Conflicting Definitions of U.S. Leadership

There is nothing wrong with "leadership" per se. The United States can and should play a leading role in a number of arenas. Washington's leadership since World War II of the global trade liberalization process, for example, has been highly constructive. Such economic leadership should continue. U.S. moral and cultural leadership—the American tradition of commitment to such ideals as democracy, individual liberty, and the other philosophical foundations of the Constitution—should also continue. Such American economic and moral leadership is both beneficial and sustainable.

> *The United States can and should play a leading role in a number of arenas.*

Today's proponents of "global leadership," however, are advocating something better described as hegemony than as leadership. Unlike moral or economic leadership, global leadership does not envision the United States' leading by example or through diplomacy. Global leadership is essentially coercive, relying on "diplomacy" backed by threats or military action.

Global leadership also entails greater responsibility than does leadership in the economic or moral and cultural arenas. U.S. leadership in trade liberalization does not make the United States responsible for countries that practice protectionism. Nor does economic leadership demand that the United States use any means necessary to maintain its leadership role. Advocates of U.S. political and military leadership, however, have a much more ambitious view of the responsibilities global leadership entails and the actions the United States is obligated to take to preserve its role as global leader.

American political and military leadership can be defined in a number of ways, but two schools of thought dominate today. One school of thought, loosely associated with the Clinton administration and the Democratic Party, advocates exercising U.S. global leadership in a multilateral context to advance humanitarian or

Wilsonian objectives. The other school of thought, loosely associated with the Republican Party, advocates unilateral U.S. leadership primarily for traditional realist—power and national security—objectives.

Multilateralism vs. Unilateralism

Clinton has said, "Unilateralism in the world that we live in is not a viable option."[5] Secretary of State Madeleine Albright has explained the administration's position more fully:

> We cannot afford to abandon either peace-keeping or a multilateral approach to solving difficult problems. As much as we would wish otherwise, conflicts are going to continue. The world is going to look to the United States for leadership. It will be in our interests to provide that leadership, but we cannot and should not bear the full burden alone.[6]

The multilateralists often condemn the unilateral approach as isolationism. Historian Arthur Schlesinger Jr.'s comment, "The isolationist impulse has risen from the grave, and it has taken the new form of unilateralism," is representative.[7]

Many Republicans, on the other hand, allege that "multilateralism [has become] something of a cover for U.S. retrenchment," in the words of Sen. Richard Lugar (R-Ind.).[8] House Majority Leader Dick Armey of Texas has warned, "The nation has gone too far in the direction of globalism and lost sight of its essential footings, and we [congressional Republicans] intend to change that."[9] Indeed, the only time unilateralists express enthusiasm about multilateralism is when it means inviting other countries to sign on to a U.S. initiative on Washington's terms, as was the case in the Persian Gulf War. As Dole explains,

> The choices facing America are not, as some in the administration would like to portray, doing something multilaterally, doing it alone, or doing nothing. These are false choices. The real choice is whether to allow international organizations to call the shots—as in Bosnia or Somalia—or to make multilateral groupings work for American interests—as in Operation Desert Storm.[10]

Global Social Worker or Global Cop?

The other major difference between the two views is the circumstances in which the United States should exercise leadership. The Democrats generally seem more comfortable leading Wilsonian crusades with idealistic objectives—promoting democracy, protecting human rights, or delivering humanitarian assistance—than with using force for traditional security agendas. Thus, they take a hard line on Haitian dictators but favor a conciliatory stance toward

North Korea. As Michael Mandelbaum of the School of Advanced International Studies at Johns Hopkins University has said of the Clinton administration's foreign policy,

> In [Somalia, Haiti, and Bosnia] the administration was preoccupied not with relations with neighboring countries, the usual subject of foreign policy, but rather with the social, political, and economic conditions within borders. It aimed to relieve the suffering caused by ethnic cleansing in Bosnia, starvation in Somalia, and oppression in Haiti. Historically, the foreign policy of the United States has centered on American interests, defined as developments that could affect the lives of American citizens. Nothing that occurred in these three countries fit that criterion. Instead, the Clinton interventions were intended to promote American values.[11]

"Historically, the foreign policy of the United States has centered on American interests, defined as developments that could affect the lives of American citizens."—**Michael Mandelbaum, John Hopkins University**

Republicans, on the other hand, tend to favor law-and-order and realpolitik leadership, advocating intervention to keep the world in line and to preserve America's status as the world's foremost military power. Instead of restoring democracy in Haiti or taking a stand against "genocide" in Bosnia, Republicans advocate tougher policies toward such international villains as North Korea and Iran. Whatever support they have given to the idea of American action in Bosnia has generally been not for humanitarian reasons but to preserve the prestige of the United States and NATO. Lugar, for example, has stated,

> The policy dispute over Bosnia is no longer just about Bosnia, but rather about allied unity and the willingness of Europeans and Americans to adjust their Cold War political and security institutions and missions to the changing geo-strategic circumstances in and around Europe. In some ways, the details of such adjustments are less important than the pressing need to demonstrate and convince politicians and publics on both sides of the Atlantic that American leadership on European security issues is both possible and advantageous for Europeans as well as for Americans.[12]

Some on the right also hint that the United States should take a more active role in policing the world generally. Lugar has argued, "We have an unparalleled opportunity to manage the world."[13] Former U.S. senator Malcolm Wallop has been more specific: "If

America's presence and purpose in the world can be doubted, if we tolerate vacuums of power, they will be filled by others, and ultimately American blood will be spilled."[14]

It is important to point out that this description of the two approaches to U.S. leadership is extremely general. There are variations within each school of thought, and the two approaches correspond only roughly to the two political parties, with numerous exceptions.[15] And other prominent advocates of U.S. global leadership do not fit into either of the schools of thought outlined here.

Joshua Muravchik of the American Enterprise Institute, for example, argues in favor of an expansive and costly version of global leadership that encompasses both Wilsonian and realist objectives. His book, *The Imperative of American Leadership*, opens with the proclamation:

> This book is an argument. It is an argument for a certain kind of U.S. foreign policy now that the Cold War is behind us. It is an argument for a foreign policy that is engaged, proactive, interventionist, and expensive.
>
> This argument flies in the face of the shibboleth that America cannot be the world's policeman. In truth, it must be more than that. A policeman gets his assignments from higher authority, but in the community of nations there is no authority higher than America. . . . America is the wealthiest, mightiest, and most respected nation. At times, it must be the policeman or head of the posse—at others, the mediator, teacher, or benefactor. In short, America must accept the role of world leader.[16]

Muravchik's vision of American global leadership transcends those of both prominent Democrats and Republicans—whose notions of U.S. leadership Muravchik criticizes as disguised isolationism.

The fundamental disagreements about what constitutes global leadership underscore the ambiguity and elasticity of the term. The policy is vulnerable to both honest misinterpretation and deliberate misrepresentation—by the U.S. foreign policy community, the American public, foreign governments, and foreign populations. It is also dangerously easy to manipulate, allowing policymakers to disguise a misguided or foundering policy as a mysterious but necessary way of exercising or preserving American leadership. Vagueness may be useful for propaganda purposes, but basing U.S. foreign policy on such shifting sands is unwise.

Translating Leadership into Policy

The ambiguity of "leadership" is also one of the reasons it is so difficult to translate into policy. At its most extreme, leadership-driven foreign policy suggests that the United States is responsible to some degree for everyone, everywhere. It is unlikely that Washington could or would seek to take the idea to that extreme in terms of policy. The inescapable dilemma, then, is how to determine which situations demand Washington's attention and which can be left to run their course.

The proponents of leadership cannot agree on the proper criteria for making such decisions. Of those who contend that the United

---

"Those who shout the loudest about genocide and war seem to care only when the victims are white Europeans."—Doug Bandow, syndicated coulumnist

---

States must exhibit leadership by protecting multiethnic Bosnia-Herzegovina against the secessionist Bosnian Serbs, for example, A. M. Rosenthal of the *New York Times* has asked, "Why only Bosnia?"

> All over the world, rebel peoples are at war with their internationally recognized governments. They die to destroy regimes they detest—or just separate from them. But in only one country has the West gone to war to block anti-government forces: in Bosnia, where the Serbian Christians seek separation from a Government they see as created and held by Serbian Muslims.[17]

Advocating U.S. intervention in the Bosnian war while ignoring other, similar regional wars is random at best. Such selectivity could, however, be perceived as having more sinister motives. Citing more deadly recent conflicts in such places as Sudan, Cambodia, Rwanda, and Angola, syndicated columnist Doug Bandow has observed, "For all of the passion exhibited by those who advocate military intervention to protect Bosnian Muslims, it seems strangely limited. Put bluntly, those who shout the loudest about genocide and war seem to care only when the victims are white Europeans."[18]

The decision about when and where to exercise American leadership—given the impossibility of applying it everywhere American values are offended—is inherently arbitrary unless it is linked to U.S. vital interests. Comments by Amb. Robert G. Neumann of the

Center for Strategic and International Studies on the difficulty of deciding when to intervene against "evil" are especially revealing on that point:

> If you decide that intervention by force is needed, a choice of where it is to be placed is always questionable and unfair, but we must not, in my opinion, prevent ourselves from acting at all because then evil really prevails. . . . You have to make a decision who are the guilty parties—never mind the details that others are guilty. There are always others guilty as well. That is an academic discussion.[19]

What Neumann dismisses as an "academic discussion" has tremendous and troubling real-world implications for those parties that are arbitrarily deemed guilty. The troubling moral implications of military action are generally accepted as a necessary evil when national security is at stake. When intervention is contemplated for essentially altruistic reasons, however—to stop "evil," for instance— it would seem that moral implications should take on considerably more importance. For the world's leading power to exercise leadership by combatting "evil" (or "ethnic cleansing," "aggression," or the like) on a random or, at the very least, highly selective basis—which will at times entail punishing innocent parties for the sins of others—is not only ironic, it more closely resembles bullying than leadership.

Promise Now, Pay Later

Another policy problem involves the grandiose rhetoric that is a hallmark of global leadership and frequently results in policy dilemmas or embarrassing backpedaling. U.S. officials too often succumb to the temptation to make extravagant promises of future U.S. action—usually at times when the likelihood of having to act on those promises seems remote (or at least beyond the next election).

Colorado College political science professor David C. Hendrickson has described the danger of lavish promises. In the 1992 presidential campaign, he writes, Clinton

> not only signed on to the idea of a "new world order," but added [other commitments] that, taken together, amounted to a considerably more ambitious agenda. He would press the Chinese on human rights by linking improvements to renewal of China's most-favored-nation trade status, bring democracy to Haiti and Cuba by tightening the trade embargoes against both, and stop Serbian aggression in Bosnia by air strikes and by opposing any settlement that seemed to reward the Serbs for their misdeeds.[20]

One of the results of Clinton's campaign rhetoric, according to Hendrickson, has been a loss of U.S. prestige abroad, "stemming from the realization in foreign capitals that American policy cannot be taken at face value or need not be taken seriously (because, as J. P. Morgan said of the market, it fluctuates)."[21]

Extravagant Promises

Hendrickson's criticism pertained to Clinton's campaign promises, but Clinton's failure to fulfill commitments he reiterated after

---

In the cases of both China and North Korea, Washington overestimated both what it needed to do and what the United States was capable of doing.

---

becoming president is considerably more troublesome. One example is Clinton's decision to link China's most-favored-nation trade status to human rights, a policy he later abandoned. As Dole criticized, "In less than two years, China—and the world—saw a complete reversal of administration policy with an intermediate stop at indecision. The Chinese leadership, our allies, and our adversaries learned an important lesson: the President of the United States does not always mean what he says."[22]

The Clinton administration also was forced to back away from overly ambitious rhetoric about the North Korean nuclear weapons program. Administration officials initially declared that North Korea would not be allowed to develop any nuclear weapons. Later, the administration conceded that Pyongyang may in fact already possess a small number of nuclear devices.[23]

In the cases of both China and North Korea, Washington overestimated both what it needed to do and what the United States was capable of doing. Human rights and nuclear nonproliferation are worthwhile goals, but they are competing with an array of other foreign policy objectives—many of which are more important. Because of China's immense market potential, trade was a higher priority than human rights. And the risks associated with forcibly denying Pyongyang a nuclear weapons capability—conducting a preemptive strike, for example—were more dangerous than North Korea's possession of a few nuclear devices. The lesson is that U.S. officials should not be seduced by the myth of Washington's omnipotence into making commitments that the United States cannot meet or does not value enough relative to other priorities to meet.

Global leadership, however, demands U.S. involvement in many issues that have little or no impact on American vital interests. Consider the ambitious set of election-year foreign policy goals Christopher, invoking U.S. leadership, set forth in early 1996. Expansion of NATO, achievement of a comprehensive test ban treaty, ratification of START II, and integration of environmental goals into diplomacy were designated as top diplomatic objectives. In addition, Christopher said, the administration would work to repair U.S. relations with China; crack down on narcotics trafficking; prosecute war criminals in Bosnia and Rwanda; end the Arab-Israeli conflict; and "pursue initiatives in such places and Northern Ireland, Haiti,

---

America cannot and must not be the world's policeman.

Cyprus, Angola, Burundi, Peru, and Ecuador."[24] As the breathtaking expansiveness of the administration's 1996 agenda suggests, foreign policy based on U.S. leadership perpetuates and encourages the myth that the United States can and should manage the rest of the world.

Wars for Credibility

Global leadership, then, requires both that the United States get involved in numerous conflicts around the globe and that it do whatever is necessary to prevail in order to preserve U.S. credibility. That is often overlooked. Hendrickson dismissed the significance of the failure of the U.S. mission in Somalia because "Somalia involved no great interest on the part of the United States; the intervention there could be abandoned with the same casualness as it was undertaken."[25] Sen. Edward M. Kennedy (D-Mass.) displayed a similar attitude during the congressional debates over the U.S. operation in the former Yugoslavia: "We all recognize the mission may fail. But the real failure would be not to try."[26]

On the contrary, if leadership is the raison d'être of American foreign policy, and especially if it is the primary rationale for a U.S. military operation, the United States must succeed, even at heavy cost, because preserving American credibility is of paramount importance. Dole stressed that point: "No more overnight reversals, no more conflicting signals, and no more strategic incoherence. Our future security depends on American leadership that is respected, American leadership that is trusted, and, when necessary, American leadership that is feared."[27] The difficulty—if not impossibility—of pursuing a policy that demands U.S. involvement in numerous affairs unrelated to American security while also requiring that the United States do whatever is necessary to succeed in all diplomatic and military endeavors it undertakes is obvious.

The Clinton administration's handling of Bosnia is a striking example of problems associated with making ill-conceived commitments to demonstrate leadership, then having to follow through to preserve credibility. When the UN Protection Force in the former Yugoslavia appeared on the verge of collapse in the spring and summer of 1995, Clinton volunteered U.S. troops to assist in its extraction on the basis of U.S. leadership of NATO: "As the leader of NATO, the United States would have an obligation . . . to assist in that withdrawal, involving thousands of U.S. troops in a difficult mission."[28]

Largely to avoid having to honor that commitment, the United States instead sent Assistant Secretary of State Richard Holbrooke to launch an ambitious peace initiative as NATO conducted robust air strikes against the Bosnian Serbs.[29] The final version of Holbrooke's peace plan, the Dayton agreement, is a convoluted measure that few experts believe will endure.[30] Nonetheless, Clinton sent U.S. troops to enforce the precarious accord. In his nationally televised address to the American people, he explained why:

> My duty as President is to match the demands for American leadership to our strategic interests and to our ability to make a difference. America cannot and must not be the world's policeman. . . . We can't do everything, but we must do what we can. There are times and places where our leadership can mean the difference between peace and war. . . . The terrible war in Bosnia is such a case. Nowhere is the need for American leadership more stark or more immediate than in Bosnia.[31]

Christopher characterized the Bosnia mission as "an acid test of American leadership."[32] Ironically, though, a U.S. failure to establish an independent, peaceful Bosnia—a highly possible outcome— would cause immeasurable damage to U.S. leadership. Holbrooke has conceded as much:

> Failure is unthinkable. We cannot afford to fail. NATO's future, the relationship of Central Europe and of Russia to the West, Germany's willingness to take on a more active role in European security, the future of the American people's support for peacekeeping and for international engagement—all of these things are at stake in Bosnia.[33]

The Imperatives of Leadership

U.S. global leadership can be a policy straitjacket even in the absence of extravagant rhetoric, creating "imperatives" where there are none. Zbigniew Brzezinski has said of Bosnia,

> [The United States is] fleeing the moral and practical imperatives of its own power. . . . You Americanize the war [in Bosnia] or you Americanize the genocide. Since the United States is the only power in the world that can stop the ethnic cleansing, the United States is responsible if the ethnic cleansing continues.[34]

Washington, to its credit, has not yet accepted responsibility for ending ethnic cleansing around the world. Brzezinski, however, seems to suggest that Washington need not explicitly agree to such a mission; the United States must stop ethnic cleansing because it (supposedly) has the ability to do so.

An Atlantic Council working group has reached similar conclusions about American responsibility with respect to ethnic conflicts. The group issued a report that conceded, "None of the ethnic tensions the Working Group analyzed in its case studies challenge American vital interests, i.e., interests which the U.S. would go to war to defend, and it would be an exceedingly rare ethnic conflict that would challenge American vital interests."[35] Nonetheless, the report went on to say, "The United States will often have responsibility to take the lead and will have a unique leadership role to play in regard to ethnic conflicts."[36] Again, the implication appears to be that the United States need not seek or accept a major role in a specific situation to incur obligations; U.S. power and the habitual claiming of the mantle of world leadership make many obligations automatic.

Given the number of ethnic conflicts that are currently raging and are likely to flare up in the near future—the Stockholm International Peace Research Institute counted 30 major armed conflicts in 1995 alone—that imperative puts too great a claim on American blood and treasure to provide the underpinning for a viable foreign policy.[37] Christopher has commented, "Our strength is a blessing, not a burden."[38] The argument that the United States must take action simply because it has the ability to do so, however, carries the implicit assumption that U.S. strength is indeed a burden rather than a blessing. For those who insist that American power automatically entails far-flung obligations, it may be worthwhile to recall John Quincy Adams's famous words:

> America goes not abroad in search of monsters to destroy. . . .

She well knows that by once enlisting under other banners than her own, were they even the banners of foreign independence, she would involve herself beyond the power of extrication, in all the wars of interest and intrigue, of individual avarice, envy, and ambition, which assumed the colors and usurped the standards of freedom. . . . She might become the dictatress of the world. She would no longer be the ruler of her own spirit.[39]

Costs of American Leadership

Global leadership is a tremendously costly proposition. The question of what resources—economic and human—Americans are willing to devote to ensuring that the United States remains the world's only superpower is seldom raised. Indeed, it is almost heretical to mention the costs of such leadership, as Mathews has pointed out: "Weirdly, to say now that America's goals should reflect our relatively diminished resources and willingness to spend them is to invite being labeled as a despised 'declinist.'"[40]

> *Leadership cannot be achieved through dollar diplomacy and impressive military spending alone.*

Leadership's Financial Price Tag

The costs, though, are real. Gingrich has admitted,

You do not need today's defense budget to defend the United States. You need today's defense budget to lead the world. If you are prepared to give up leading the world, you can have a much smaller defense budget.[41]

The U.S. defense budget today totals approximately $265 billion—more than $1,000 each year for every American and more than the combined defense budgets of the other industrial powers.[42] A significant proportion of that spending is linked to American security commitments around the world. NATO costs U.S. taxpayers approximately $60 billion to $90 billion per year; U.S. commitments to Japan, South Korea, and other East Asian allies cost approximately $35 billion to $40 billion per year; and the American commitment to the Persian Gulf region costs at least $40 billion per year.[43] Those commitments, which total between $135 billion and $170 billion annually, are in place largely to preserve American leadership.

Other major powers, concerned about preserving their own security but not preoccupied with notions of global leadership, spend far less. Consider the 1995 defense budgets of NATO's leading European powers: France, $40.5 billion; Germany, $34.02 billion; and

Great Britain, $34.48 billion.[44] Despite the war in the former Yugo-slavia and the potential for unrest throughout the former Soviet Union, which have a considerably greater impact on European interests than on American interests, European members of NATO spend only a fraction of what Washington spends. There is a similar pattern in East Asia, where Japan's 1995 defense budget was only $53.8 billion and South Korea's 1995 budget an anemic $14.36 billion, despite the North Korean threat and other tensions throughout the region.[45] In the absence of any threat to U.S. vital interests, burdening American taxpayers with a $265 billion defense budget is a high price to pay for "global leadership."

> *"We can't lead if we don't put our own people at risk."*— **Thomas Friedman, the** *New York Times*

Blood Sacrifices

Human costs must also be considered. Leadership cannot be achieved through dollar diplomacy and impressive military spending alone. U.S. troops sometimes will have to go into battle to prove American prowess. The American public has demonstrated a meager tolerance of American casualties, especially since the remarkably low body count in the Gulf War seemed to suggest that a war could be fought with little bloodshed.

That aversion to human loss has been the object of considerable criticism. Thomas Friedman, foreign affairs columnist for the *New York Times*, has complained,

> We can't lead if we don't put our own people at risk, but few . . . postmodern crises offer the sort of compelling moral or strategic appeal that Presidents traditionally use to justify putting American soldiers in harm's way. Nor do these crises offer the hope of quick, bloodless, video-arcade solutions, à la the gulf war. This is a key reason the Western alliance seems so leaderless in facing the new crises of today.[46]

But the evidence suggests that the American public is not averse to military casualties for the sake of defending vital American interests. The public is intolerant of battlefield losses in military operations that appear to have little or no direct link to U.S. national security. As David Evans of Business Executives for National Security has observed, "The issue really takes on additional sensitivity when there is not a clear and compelling national interest for the government to impose the blood tax on its youth."[47] And, as Friedman conceded, today's crises do not offer the "compelling moral or strategic appeal" that would raise American tolerance for spilled blood. Public skepticism about sending U.S. troops to Bosnia is consistent with this analysis; polls have indicated that Americans do not believe U.S. vital interests are at stake, and consequently support for the operation is weak.[48]

The Alleged Benefits of U.S. Leadership: Burden Sharing and Diplomatic Achievements

Given the enormous economic and human costs and the troublesome policy implications associated with leading the world, the supposed benefits of leadership deserve close scrutiny. One alleged benefit is that the United States, by taking the lead, can persuade the rest of the world to pay for and accept some of the risks of foreign policy initiatives that the United States would otherwise pursue alone.

The Burden-Sharing Illusion

The preeminent example of such burden sharing is the gulf war. Much of the foreign policy community agrees that Iraq's invasion of Kuwait and threats to Saudi Arabia posed an intolerable risk to U.S. national security and that therefore the United States would have and should have gone to war over the matter with or without assistance from other countries. But because of President Bush's adroit display of U.S. leadership, it is said, the United States was able to gain the cooperation and financial support of other countries. Former Reagan and Clinton administration official David Gergen has written,

> The president wisely decided to internationalize the opposition to Iraq. While it was obvious that the United States was calling the shots, the fact that the UN Security Council gave its blessing to American policy at each step along the way provided a stamp of international legitimacy. . . . the fact that other members of the coalition were willing to defray the costs borne by U.S. taxpayers also made the effort much more appealing.[49]

As Foreign Policy editor Charles William Maynes noted at the time of the crisis, however, international support was not freely given. Washington provided economic aid to the Soviet Union; forgave Egypt's debt; and ignored human rights abuses in China, Ethiopia, and Syria.[50] Moreover, Japan and the West European powers had a significant interest of their own at risk—gulf oil, on which those countries rely far more than does the United States. Their meager contributions to the U.S.-led military operation against Saddam Hussein were not burden sharing; on the contrary, Japan and Western Europe were "free riding" on U.S. efforts in order to preserve their own security interests during the gulf war.[51]

An Invitation to Free Riders

The free-rider problem has long been an issue in U.S. security relations with its allies. Early in the Cold War Washington made massive security commitments to Western Europe, Japan, and South Korea. In light of those countries' postwar economic and military weakness—which the Soviet Union almost certainly would have exploited—those commitments were justifiable in the context of U.S. interests. Today, however, given the demise of the Soviet Union and the economic strength of Washington's NATO and East Asian allies, there is no reason for American taxpayers to underwrite those countries' security.

"The maintenance of a strong U.S. commitment to post-Cold War Europe benefits [the United States and France]."—**Pierre Lellouche, member of the French cabinet**

Yet even as they cut their own defense budgets, U.S. allies insist that the American contribution to their defense—the presence of U.S. troops and (appealing to the vanity of American policymakers) Washington's political leadership—is indispensable to their security. The French, for example, are notorious for having resented Washington's dominance of European security throughout the Cold War, and they still insist on the need for a strong European defense identity independent of the United States. Paris has nonetheless made clear that Washington must never abandon its obligations to European security. As Pierre Lellouche, a member of the cabinet of French president Jacques Chirac (who, within his first year in office, announced dramatic cuts in defense spending) has emphasized,

> The maintenance of a strong U.S. commitment to post-Cold War Europe benefits both countries [the United States and France]. The United States needs to remain strongly attached to Europe for its own political, economic, and strategic interests. . . . France needs a strong American commitment to the post-Cold War Europe in which nationalism, border questions, and structural imbalances have been resuscitated.[52]

Other European NATO members, many of which are also cutting their defense budgets, have made similar protestations of their inability to provide for their security without U.S. assistance—as have Japan and South Korea. By doing so, they flatter the United States into paying defense-related costs they would otherwise have to assume.

The argument that, because of U.S. leadership, Washington can secure international cooperation and assistance for activities that the United States would otherwise undertake and pay for alone is false. The reality is that America's leadership role enables other powers to transfer costs and risks to the United States.

Leadership and Diplomatic Successes

Specific diplomatic achievements are also sometimes cited as benefits of U.S. political and military leadership. But the link between a successful diplomatic initiative and U.S. leadership is often tenuous or nonexistent. Clinton has boasted of "the benefits of America's leadership at the White House [in October 1995] where leaders from all over the Middle East gathered to support the agreement between Israel and the Palestinian Authority."[53] But, as syndicated columnist and former National Security Council staffer Stefan Halper has pointed out, "If anyone has the right to claim credit for the current state of Arab-Israeli relations, it is the Norwegians—who negotiated the agreement—not us."[54]

Indeed, despite Herculean efforts by every U.S. president since Carter, Israel and the Palestinians were unable to make concrete progress toward peace until the United States got out of the way. Not only was the agreement reached without U.S. leadership, the evidence suggests that negotiations would have been fruitless as long as Washington ran the show. The scrutiny that accompanies high-profile American diplomatic initiatives is often more than delicate negotiations can withstand. In the past, U.S.-sponsored Arab-Israeli peace talks often got derailed on procedural matters, whose importance was magnified by U.S. officials and Washington's media establishment. It was only in the relative obscurity of Norway, free from the pressure of negotiating under the auspices of the world's leading power, that symbolism could be put aside so that substantive negotiations could take place.

It is important to point out, too, that the Middle East peace agreements probably owe more to the end of the Cold War than to the brilliance of Norwegian or U.S. diplomacy. If the Arabs and Israelis could have continued their Cold War practice of exploiting the U.S.-Soviet rivalry—in particular, if the Arab states had not lost Soviet military and economic patronage—peace agreements might not have been signed. Absent the powerful motive of self-interest, any amount of leadership from an outside party would probably not have had a decisive impact on negotiations.

Nor does U.S. leadership guarantee that the peace agreements will endure. Washington has been unable to end violence since the peace agreements were signed, although Clinton administration officials have made numerous attempts to do so. Until the parties themselves decide that genuine peace is worthwhile, there is little the United States can do.

A World without U.S. Leadership: The Myth of the Impending Apocalypse

Other proponents of U.S. political and military leadership do not point to particular benefits; instead, they warn of near-certain disaster if the United States relinquishes its leadership role. Christopher paints a bleak picture:

> Just consider what the world would be like without American leadership in the last two years alone. We would have four nuclear states in the former Soviet Union, instead of one, with Russian missiles still targeted at our homes. We would have a full-throttled nuclear program in North Korea; no GATT agreement and no NAFTA; brutal dictators still terrorizing Haiti; very likely, Iraqi troops back in Kuwait; and an unresolved Mexican economic crisis, which would threaten stability at our border.[55]

External powers usually lack the means to prevent or end civil wars.

Gingrich has pronounced a future without American leadership "a big mess."[56] And former British prime minister Margaret Thatcher has warned,

> What we are possibly looking at in 2095 [absent U.S. leadership] is an unstable world in which there are more than half a dozen "great powers," each with its own clients, all vulnerable if they stand alone, all capable of increasing their power and influence if they form the right kind of alliance, and all engaged willy-nilly in perpetual diplomatic maneuvers to ensure that their relative positions improve rather than deteriorate. In other words, 2095 might look like 1914 played on a somewhat larger stage.[57]

In other words, if America abdicates its role as world leader, we are condemned to repeat the biggest mistakes of the 20th century—or perhaps do something even worse.

Such thinking is seriously flawed, however. First, to assert that U.S. leadership can stave off otherwise inevitable global chaos vastly overestimates the power of any single country to influence world events. The United States is powerful, but it still can claim only 5 percent of the world's population and 20 percent of world economic output. Moreover, regardless of the resources Americans might be willing to devote to leading the world, today's problems often do not lend themselves well to external solutions. As Maynes has pointed out,

Today, the greatest fear of most states is not external aggression but internal disorder. The United States can do little about the latter, whereas it used to be able to do a great deal about the former. In other words, the coinage of U.S. power in the world has been devalued by the change in the international agenda.[58]

Indeed, many of the foreign policy problems that have confounded Washington since the demise of the Soviet Union are the kinds of problems that are likely to trouble the world well into the next century.

"Failed states," such as Somalia, may not be uncommon. But, as the ill-fated U.S. and UN operations in that country showed, there

---

Instead of trying to lead the world, the United States should concentrate on the protection of its vital national security interests.

---

is very little that outside powers can do about such problems. External powers usually lack the means to prevent or end civil wars, such as those in Rwanda and the former Yugoslavia, unless they are willing to make a tremendous effort to do so. Yet those types of internecine conflicts are likely to be one of the primary sources of international disorder for the foreseeable future.

Despite the doomsayers who prophesy global chaos in the absence of U.S. leadership, however, Washington's limited ability to dampen such conflicts is not cause for panic. Instability is a normal feature of an international system of sovereign states, which the United States can tolerate and has tolerated for more than two centuries. If vital American interests are not at stake, instability itself becomes a serious problem only if the United States blunders into it, as it did in Somalia and Bosnia.[59]

Toward a Sustainable Foreign Policy

The nebulous benefits of U.S. global leadership do not justify its immense costs, and it is unlikely that the United States is even capable of pursuing such a strategy over the long term. Scholars Jonathan Clarke and James Clad have observed, "As American leverage in the world (aid, effective military power, or diplomatic sway) continues to decline, America increases its conditions and demands. . . . Such bluster counts for little."[60] And while trying to lead the world is costly enough now, a strategy that holds as its highest objective the exercise and preservation of American leader-ship seems likely to lead inexorably to an increase in commitments and costs over the long term.

Instead of trying to lead the world, the United States should con-centrate on the protection of its vital national security interests. It can do so better by behaving as the "first among equals" in the com-munity of great powers than by insisting that the United States, as the world's only superpower, can and should take responsibility for events all over the globe. Great power status does, after all, confer not only the ability to get involved in conflicts around the world but also the power to remain aloof from lesser quarrels.

It is conceivable, for example, that Macedonia or Albania could have been drawn involuntarily into the Balkan war if Serbia had been intent on widening the war. It is much more difficult to envi-sion more powerful European countries, such as Germany or France, being drawn into the conflict against their will. Ill-conceived intervention by Germany or France (or the United States, for that matter) could trap any of those countries in a Balkan quagmire, but a scenario in which Serbia or some other Balkan power could force any of those countries to enter the war is difficult to imagine.

American strength is important, but strength is far more than mil-itary or diplomacy budgets. The largest military and diplomatic establishments in the world are useless if they are not used prop-erly. Political strength—credibility—is also crucial. Policies under-taken on the basis of abstract ideas of American leadership are unlikely to enjoy much credibility around the world. Even though Washington may not always back down from overly ambitious rhet-oric, potential adversaries will be more inclined to take their chances if the United States develops a record of making empty threats and promises.

A national security strategy based on the protection of U.S. vital interests would be far more credible. The United States would then have no reason to make promises or threats it did not fully intend to keep. In the relatively unlikely event that the United States were to face a challenge to its vital interests, a potential adversary would be taking a grave risk if it chose to disregard warnings from Washing-ton, given the certainty of the United States' responding immedi-ately and strongly to any trespass. Ideally, U.S. credibility and strength would be adequate to counter potential threats without military action. In the event that military action were required to defend U.S. national security interests, however, such action would probably command the support of Congress and the American pub-lic. As is evident from the debate over Bosnia, military action for the sake of U.S. leadership does not command that support.

A World without U.S. Military Leadership

If Washington renounces world leadership, is the United States condemned to stand idly by while villains and irredentists around the world terrorize helpless populations? It is unfortunate but true that brutal civil or subregional conflicts are likely to mar the future—as they do the present and have the past. There are many nasty parochial wars that simply cannot be settled by outside powers at an acceptable cost to those powers, whether or not the United States claims the mantle of world leadership.

A more critical issue is the evolution of the international system after U.S. hegemony. Washington can exert considerable influence (though not full control) over the development of that system. Although a number of different scenarios may be acceptable to the United States, Washington should make certain that any global system that succeeds American hegemony has two important characteristics. First, international power and responsibility must be decentralized; the transfer of U.S. global influence and responsibilities to another state, alliance, or global organization such as the United Nations should not be permitted. It is as unrealistic to base the international system on the illusion that some other country or international organization can effectively lead the world as it is to depend on U.S. global leadership. Second, the international system must include a means of checking aspiring hegemons.

Regional Security Organizations

Such a system could take several forms. One possibility is the strengthening of regional security organizations, such as the Western European Union. Regional security organizations are an effective way of keeping order among member states and can also take care of contingencies in their general areas. Had the European countries not been so dependent on NATO, for example, the WEU should have been able to subdue the crisis in the former Yugoslavia if the conflict had been perceived as a wider threat to Europe. Regional organizations could also serve as potential partners to the United States in the event of a serious threat to their mutual interests elsewhere in the world.

Unfortunately, regional security organizations require a high degree of cohesion among member states and therefore are not possible in many parts of the world. The WEU is probably the only such organization that is viable in the near future, although effective regional security organizations encompassing some Latin American and Asian countries are not inconceivable. In much of the rest of the world, however, there is little evidence of the cohesion and common interest that would be a precondition for a functioning regional security organization.

Spheres of Influence

An alternative to regional security organizations is the creation of spheres of influence. The notion of spheres of influence has in the past carried a rather sinister connotation and could still be troublesome if a dominant regional power sought to subvert its neighbors, especially if it subsequently aspired to challenge other major powers. But as long as dominant powers restrict their activities to typical "great power" behavior—which would generally mean shoring up security and prestige but not expansionism—there is nothing inherently evil about spheres of influence.

Several prominent foreign policy scholars have pointed out the feasibility of spheres of influence. Ronald Steel of the University of Southern California has written,

> Regional disturbances that do not threaten the world power balance should be dealt with by the major powers of the region, ideally with the endorsement of the international community. Instead of seeking an ephemeral global security, we should, as Charles William Maynes has argued in *Foreign Policy*, encourage a policy of "regional self-reliance [that] would recognize that certain powerful states in each area will inevitably play a special security role." In other words, we must accept the reality of the longstanding tradition of spheres of influence—a tradition that we scrupulously insist upon in the Western Hemisphere under our unilaterally imposed Monroe Doctrine.[61]

Spheres of influence make sense because the world's major powers have an interest in, and usually the ability to maintain a degree of order in, their regions. There is always some risk that the leading power in a particular sphere of influence may abuse its position or develop expansionist ambitions. The decentralization of international power, however, should ensure that the United States, other major powers, or regional security organizations—acting alone or in concert—could check unacceptable behavior on the part of a dominant regional power.

Balance of Power

Yet another alternative is the establishment of regional balance-of-power arrangements, which may be appropriate in the Middle East, for example. There are serious obstacles to the creation of a viable regional security organization in that area—as demonstrated by the problems the Gulf Cooperation Council has faced—and there is no clear dominant power around which a sphere of influence is likely to develop. Instead, the locus of power tends to shift among the larger states. The United States has in the past sought to manipulate the balance of power by bolstering certain countries as a means of checking others. That risky strategy had disastrous consequences with respect to Iran and Iraq, and, given the unpopularity of the regimes in Egypt and Saudi Arabia and those regimes' close identification with Washington, it may well backfire again.

Allowing the balance of power in the region to evolve without U.S. interference would help shield the United States from the consequences of violent and sudden shifts in the balance but could still be expected to prevent a regional hegemon from rising. As University of Chicago political scientist Stephen M. Walt pointed out in *The Origins of Alliances*,

> Compared with the other hypotheses examined in this book, the general hypothesis that states choose allies in order to balance against the most serious threat was the clear winner. Its merits were shown in two important ways. First, balancing was far more common than bandwagoning, and bandwagoning was almost always confined to especially weak and isolated states. Second, the importance of ideological distinction declined as the level of threat increased; ideological solidarity was most powerful when security was high or when ideological factors and security considerations reinforced each other.[62]

The tendency of states to balance against a prospective hegemon, instead of "bandwagoning," has been evident in the Middle East. As Walt observed, "Despite the fact that the Middle East lacks an established tradition of balance of power statecraft . . . , the advantages of seeking allies in order to balance against threats have obviously been apparent to the various actors in the Middle East. . . . the ascendancy of ambitious regional powers (such as Iraq under Nuri al-Said and Egypt under Nasser) consistently led other regional actors to join forces . . . to resist the attempt."[63]

The strategic environment of the Middle East of the 1990s remains conducive to balancing, as an assortment of similarly sized powers—Egypt, Syria, Saudi Arabia, Iraq, and Iran—continue to share an interest in preventing the rise of any single power to primacy. The United States may have to tolerate a degree of instability as power shifts among those states, but American vital interests should be reasonably safe as long as power remains diffused throughout the region. If a hegemon were to arise, especially if it were clearly hostile to U.S. interests, the United States would still have the option of acting alone or joining forces with European and other powers to deal with that problem.

Rational Change Now or Involuntary Change Later?

The United States cannot dictate the precise nature of the global system that succeeds U.S. hegemony, but it can exert considerable influence. In the final analysis, any of the above scenarios, or a combination of them—say, a stronger WEU in Europe and spheres of influence or regional balance-of-power arrangements in other regions—should be tolerable. As long as no single power or group of powers emerges with the capability and intent to challenge U.S. vital interests, the United States should be reasonably secure. To further enhance its security, the United States should always maintain sufficient military strength so that it could influence the distribution of power if serious imbalances were to arise. It should do so as a balancer of last resort, however, and allow smaller scale shifts to be addressed at the regional level.

There are risks associated with any of the above scenarios, to be sure, but a strategy of U.S. global leadership entails an equally high or even higher level of risk and much higher costs. Moreover, it is probably unsustainable in the long term.

If the United States makes the transition to a sustainable foreign policy in the near future, it should be able to do so on its own terms. By ceding extraneous global responsibilities in a reasoned and orderly fashion, Washington will be in a good position to influence the redistribution of global power. Conversely, policymakers can continue to pursue a world leadership strategy and face the crises that are likely to result from that overextension. When such crises arise, the United States may be forced to make abrupt shifts in policy and may have little ability to influence the subsequent redistribution of power and responsibility in the international system. The benefits of voluntarily scaling back American global responsibilities sooner instead of being forced to do so later are obvious. It is not a formula for utopia, but it is far more realistic than a crusade to lead the world.

Notes

1. Warren Christopher, "America's Leadership, America's Opportunity," *Foreign Policy 98* (Spring 1995): 8.

2. Robert Dole, "Shaping America's Global Future," *Foreign Policy 98* (Spring 1995): 36.

3. Newt Gingrich, "Remarks Delivered at Center for Strategic and International Studies," Washington, July 18, 1995, Federal News Service transcript, p. 6.

4. Jessica Mathews, "What It Means to Lead," *Washington Post*, March 13, 1995, p. A15.

5. Bill Clinton, "Remarks to Freedom House," October 6, 1995, White House, Office of the Press Secretary, p. 9.

6. Madeleine Albright, "Building a Consensus on International Peace-keeping," Statement before the Senate Foreign Relations Committee, October 20, 1993, U.S. Department of State Dispatch 4, no. 46 (November 15, 1993): 792.

7. Arthur Schlesinger Jr. "Back to the Womb?" *Foreign Affairs 74*, no. 4 (July-August 1995): 5.

8. Quoted in Robert S. Greenberger, "As Global Crises Mount, More Americans Want America to Stay Home," *Wall Street Journal*, October 28, 1993, p. A1.

9. Quoted in Eric Schmitt, "House Votes Bill to Cut U.N. Funds for Peacekeeping," *New York Times*, February 17, 1995, p. A9.

10. Dole, "Shaping America's Global Future," p. 37. Emphasis in original.

11. Michael Mandelbaum, "Foreign Policy as Social Work," *Foreign Affairs 75*, no. 1 (January-February 1996): 17.

12. Richard G. Lugar, "NATO: Out of Area or Out of Business: A Call for U.S. Leadership to Revive and Redefine the Alliance," Remarks delivered to the Open Forum of the U.S. Department of State, August 2, 1993, Press release, p. 1.

13. Quoted in "Lugar: Let States Manage Safety Net," *USA Today*, January 4, 1996, p. 9A.

14. Malcolm Wallop, "Beyond the Water's Edge," *Policy Review 74* (Fall 1995): 70.

15. For example, Rep. Sam Nunn (D-Ga.) is often closely identified with Lugar on foreign policy matters; Sen. Nancy Landon Kassebaum (R-Kans.) is less hostile than most Republicans and conservatives to allowing U.S. troops to serve under UN command, while Rep. Lee Hamilton (D-Ind.) is somewhat more critical of the United Nations generally than are most of his Democratic colleagues. Eighteen House Democrats voted for the National Security Revitalization Act, part of the GOP "Contract with America," while four House Republicans voted against it. Those are only a few of the exceptions to the Republican/Democratic approaches described in this analysis.

16. Joshua Muravchik, *The Imperative of American Leadership* (Washington: American Enterprise Institute, 1996), p. 1.

17. A. M. Rosenthal, "Why Only Bosnia?" *New York Times*, May 30, 1995, p. A17.

18. Doug Bandow, "Why Are We in Bosnia?" *Human Events 51*, no. 35 (September 15, 1995): 7.

19. Robert G. Neumann, "Peace-Imposing Intervention," in *U.S. National Interests in the 21st Century*, Proceedings of a conference organized by the DACOR Bacon House Foundation, Washington, October 7, 1994, ed. Robin M. Gurley (Washington: Diplomatic and Consular Officers Retired, n.d.), p. 78.

20. David C. Hendrickson, "The Recovery of Internationalism," *Foreign Affairs 73*, no. 4 (September-October 1994): 27.

21. Ibid., pp. 27-28.

22. Robert Dole, "America and Asia: Restoring U.S. Leadership in the Pacific," Remarks delivered at the Center for Strategic and International Studies, Washington, May 9, 1996, p. 3.

23. Hendrickson, p. 34.

24. Quoted in Ibid.

25. Ibid., p. 39.

26. Quoted in "Impassioned Words in the Senate: National Interest or Deadly Quagmire?" *New York Times*, December 14, 1995, p. A14.

27. Dole, "America and Asia," p. 5.

28. Bill Clinton, "The Risk of 'Americanizing' the War," *Newsweek*, August 7, 1995, p. 40.

29. Officially, the air strikes were unrelated to the peace negotiations, but as Roberts Owen, the lawyer in Holbrooke's delegation, admitted, "There is no question in my mind that we bombed the Serbs to the bargaining table." Quoted in Roger Cohen, "Taming the Bullies of Bosnia," *New York Times Magazine*, December 17, 1995, p. 78.

30. The peace-enforcement mission in Bosnia is a highly uncertain enterprise. As a *Washington Post* editorial put it, "The leaders of Serbia and Croatia and of Bosnia's Serbs and Croats are extreme nationalist and irredentist politicians. It was always a long shot that they would keep open the idea of an independent Bosnia—this was the core political idea of the Dayton accord. Still, it was worth it—it was right—for outside actors to take a chance and to try to end the slaughter and the ethnic cleansing." "Dayton II," *Washington Post*, February 20, 1996, p. A10.

31. "Clinton's Words on Mission to Bosnia: 'The Right Thing to Do,'" *New York Times*, November 28, 1995, p. A14.

32. Warren Christopher, "Bosnia: An Acid Test of U.S. Leadership," U.S. Department of State Dispatch 6, no. 48 (November 27, 1995): 870.

33. Quoted in Jim Hoagland, "To Holbrooke, It's Goodbye for Now," *Washington Post*, February 25, 1996, p. C11.

34. Quoted in George Will, "Worthy of Contempt," *Washington Post*, August 3, 1995, p. A31.

35. Atlantic Council of the United States, "Ethnic Conflicts: Old Challenges, New Dimensions," July 1995, pp. 21-22.

36. Ibid., p. 22.

37. See Stockholm International Peace Research Institute, "SIPRI Yearbook 1996," Press release, June 13, 1996.

38. Warren Christopher, "Leadership for the Next American Century," Address at the John F. Kennedy School of Government, Harvard University, Cambridge, Mass., January 18, 1996.

39. Quoted in George F. Kennan, "On American Principles," *Foreign Affairs 74*, no. 2 (March-April 1995): 118.

40. Mathews, p. A15.

41. Gingrich, p. 10.

42. For fuller critiques of the size of the post-Cold War defense budget, see Lawrence Korb, "Shock Therapy for the Pentagon," *New York Times*, February 15, 1994, p. A21; and "The Military Budget," *Cato Handbook for Congress: 104th Congress* (Washington: Cato Institute, 1995).

43. Ibid., p. 102.

44. International Institute for Strategic Studies, *The Military Balance 1995/96* (Oxford: Oxford University Press, 1995), pp. 44, 48, 64.

45. Ibid., pp. 181, 185.

46. Thomas L. Friedman, "The No-Dead War," *New York Times*, August 23, 1995, p. A24.

47. Quoted in Chris Black, "U.S. Options Seen As Fewer As Military Avoids Risk," *Boston Globe*, July 23, 1995, p. 12.

48. For examples of the polling data on Bosnia, see "Opinion Outlook: Views on National Security," *National Journal*, December 23, 1995, p. 3174; and Elaine Sciolino, "Soldiering On, without an Enemy," *New York Times*, October 29, 1995, p. E1.

49. David Gergen, "America's Missed Opportunities," America and the World 1991/92, *Foreign Affairs 71*, no. 1 (1992): 6.

50. Charles William Maynes, "Dateline Washington: A Necessary War?" *Foreign Policy 82* (Spring 1991): 165.

51. For a more detailed discussion of the benefits the European powers derive from U.S. security efforts in the Persian Gulf, see Shibley Telhami and Michael O'Hanlon, "Europe's Oil, Our Troops," *New York Times*, December 30, 1995, p. A27.

52. Pierre Lellouche, "France in Search of Security," *Foreign Affairs 72*, no. 2 (Spring 1993): 130.

53. Clinton, p. 2.

54. Stefan Halper, "GOP's Policy Hiatus," *Washington Times*, October 19, 1995, p. A17.

55. Warren Christopher, "Overview of the FY 1996 International Affairs Budget," U.S. Department of State Dispatch 6, no. 7 (February 13, 1995): p. 85.

56. Gingrich, p. 4.

57. Margaret Thatcher, "Why America Must Remain Number One," *National Review*, July 31, 1995, p. 25.

58. Charles William Maynes, "What the United States Must Do to Regain the Respect of the World," *Philadelphia Inquirer*, April 14, 1995, p. 23.

59. For more detailed analysis of the global stability issue, see Barbara Conry, "The Futility of U.S. Intervention in Regional Conflicts," *Cato Institute Policy Analysis no. 209*, May 19, 1994.

60. Jonathan Clarke and James Clad, "Demented Uncle Sam," *Washington Post*, June 18, 1995, p. C4.

61. Ronald Steel, "The Domestic Core of Foreign Policy," *Atlantic Monthly*, June 1995, p. 92.

62. Stephen M. Walt, *The Origins of Alliances* (Ithaca, N.Y.: Cornell University Press, 1986), p. 263.

63. Ibid., p. 152.

The 900-Pound Gorilla[3]

NEWSDAY, FEBRUARY 18, 2001

It's not easy or comfortable being the only superpower. President George W. Bush could do just about anything he wanted in the world, but he knows he can't if he wants to live up to his own campaign pledge to fashion the role of the United States into that of a "humble superpower."

When the biggest beast in the room makes the smallest move, every other creature feels it; some are crushed even by an unintentional twitch. Like it or not, the United States is the target of envy and distrust among allies and adversaries alike.

How is Bush going to handle that? If Friday's surprise air strike on Iraq is an early indication, not with much humility or patience, at least on some red-flag issues. But Iraq is sui generis a grudge match for the Bush clan: The bombing was ordered close to the 10th anniversary of the Gulf War that failed to get rid of Saddam Hussein.

On other less urgent foreign policy issues, Bush should be expected to act much more cautiously, with the help of a formidable foreign-policy team that is long on experience and savvy.

But even this early in his administration, some contradictions are emerging that could spell trouble in the future. He is pushing for major changes in military and security policies that are making our allies uneasy and straining relations with other major powers.

Perhaps the single biggest problem Bush faces is what could become a self-inflicted wound: his insistence on deploying a national missile-defense system—NMD for short—that is technologically unproven, fearsomely expensive, and could cause needless damage to our relations with our European allies, with Russia and with China.

The NMD ploy could become the tail that wags Bush's foreign-policy dog, carrying all sorts of unintended diplomatic consequences. It could result in a serious split within the Atlantic alliance, whose European partners are deeply skeptical of Bush's NMD plans. And Europeans may use their strong opposition to NMD to dissuade Bush from diminishing U.S. military involvement in the Balkans—a mission the Europeans won't carry out alone.

---

3. Article from *Newsday* February 18, 2001. Copyright © 2001 Newsday, Inc. Reprinted with permission.

How Missile Defense Destabilizes

Perhaps more important, NMD could cause serious rifts with Russia and China. Russia would see Washington's unilateral pullout from the Anti-Ballistic Missile Treaty as a provocation. China isn't buying the argument that NMD would be designed to protect the United States from isolated attacks by a rogue state like Iraq or North Korea. Instead, Beijing would see NMD as a way to make a mockery of the Chinese nuclear deterrent—little more than a dozen intercontinental ballistic missiles—and an act that would force it into an expensive and destabilizing arms build-up in an effort to overwhelm the NMD's potential capabilities. Just as crucial, China

Bush's world won't be the same as Bill Clinton's.

fears that NMD could be used to protect not just America but Taiwan. At this point, China can dissuade Taiwan from independence only with threat of ballistic missiles, not with a conventional invasion. Feeling shorn of that threat could make China a much more difficult player to deal with, not only in East Asia but also on the international stage.

Those are steep diplomatic and political costs for the fulfillment of a campaign promise to broaden the NMD plan, which Clinton had already put into motion at a more modest level with equally tenuous justification. And though it's unlikely that Bush will be deterred from going ahead with it, he would be well advised to slow down the deployment at least until the technology proves it can work without fail. That could take years. By that time, Bush might have worked out diplomatic accommodations with Russia and China. But to act on it unilaterally and too soon is a thoroughly bad idea that could cast a disturbing shadow on all the rest of Bush's nascent foreign policies.

Bush's Policies Unlike Clinton's

Bush's world won't be the same as Bill Clinton's. His outlook on the threats and opportunities the nation faces and his notions of the United States' role are quite different. That much we know already. Where Clinton sought intense involvement as "the indispensable nation" in issues that affected vital national interests only marginally, Bush wants less. Where Clinton pushed for the propagation of the nation's values in other societies, Bush wants to maintain a greater, more respectful, distance.

Most important, where Clinton relied on a distinctly weak team of players, Bush has assembled an impressive team of foreign-policy managers. Whatever their philosophical and conceptual differences—and there are some fairly deep ones among them—experience and solid reputations characterize Secretary of State Colin Powell, Secretary of Defense Donald Rumsfeld and National Security Adviser Condoleezza Rice. Add to them Vice President Dick Cheney, a former defense secretary with strong personal ties to foreign leaders, and you have a formidable array of foreign-policy makers.

They may not always agree, however.

Powell is far more sensitive to the needs to maintain close ties to allies, improve relations with Russia and China, and be less hasty in a desire to disengage from current military commitments, such as the one in the Balkans. Rumsfeld and Rice see little need to pay much attention to Russia's sensitivities and cast China in the role of future antagonist rather than strategic partner. Powell's reluctance to engage in military involvements unless vital national interests are at stake was shaped by his Vietnam experiences, much as Rumsfeld's more hard-line views were forged in the Cold War. In most instances, however, they and Bush are likely to make pragmatic choices based on individual circumstances.

None is an out-and-out ideologue, and that's good in the turbulent world they will face:

The Middle East. Bush has no choice here. He must stay engaged. Powell's early hints that the United States would distance itself from the Israeli-Palestinian conflict was immediately belied by the speed with which he and Bush contacted both sides once the cycle of violence resumed with unabated ferocity after the Israeli election. Reviving the peace process is critical and will need intense U.S. mediation.

Iraq. It's unfinished business for Bush, Powell and Cheney, and Friday's air strike let Saddam know that they will have no patience with even the slightest provocation. They intend to take a much harder line on Iraqi intransigence, as they should. Grossly neglected by Clinton, a consensus among Gulf War allies needs to be restored on forcing Iraq to accept international arms inspections again in exchange for normalized relations. ·

China. This needs careful nuance, not a sledge-hammer approach. China cannot be cast as an inevitable adversary, but it will always be a difficult competitor deserving of wary respect. China wants a predictable relationship, which it didn't get with Clinton. Harping on human rights won't do much good, but insisting on compliance with arms controls and trade deals will.

Russia. President Vladimir Putin is becoming more assertive and less willing to cooperate with the West. Bush shouldn't give him reasons to forge closer ties with China—something that NMD could do.

Latin America. Bush is making a welcome change, starting with his trip to Mexico, by focusing more strongly on this key region. Brazil may be the key to stability and stronger trade relations. The big trouble spot: Colombia, its drug-financed civil war and the massive military aid Washington is pouring into it.

Terrorism. This is not, so far, on the Bush radar screen, and it ought to be, along with new threats—cyberterrorism, biological warfare, economic instability and disease. Threats have changed since the Cold War, but the instruments to deal with them haven't. Bush is doing the right thing by forcing a thorough rethinking of the Pentagon's weapons systems and doctrines. The same should be done with the intelligence establishment.

Bush inherited from the previous administration a set of foreign policies that—with the signal exception of the successful expansion of free trade—were at best scattershot and at worst incoherent. As he prepares to craft his own, the new president should aim for coherence, an integration of national goals with international responsibilities, and a balance between maintaining essential security and intervening abroad where we must.

But, above all, Bush should keep in mind his own injunction on humility. He can make sure that the United States is not perceived as arrogant and insensitive. And he can do that by abjuring ill-considered unilateral actions that will cast doubt on the wisdom and the reliability of the 900-pound gorilla in the room.

Bush Aides Cite "Realism" In Tougher Foreign Policy[4]

By BOB DEANS
ATLANTA JOURNAL-CONSTITUTION, MARCH 25, 2001

In just three weeks, President Bush has expelled the largest contingent of Russian agents in 15 years, rattled China with talk of advanced weapons sales to Taiwan and served notice that diplomacy will take a back seat to deterrence in his dealings with North Korea.

The Cold War is still over, but White House aides insist the tough line Bush is taking toward former U.S. adversaries is part of a new "realism" he hopes to inject into American foreign policy.

Whether the issue is Russian spies, Chinese chest-pounding across the Taiwan Straits or North Korea's alleged ballistic missile program, Bush is signaling that not all is well in U.S. relations with former Communist foes many had hoped would become American partners in the age of globalization.

"The message the president is sending is that his foreign policy is going to be based on reality," White House spokesman Ari Fleischer said Thursday. "He's going to have a realistic approach to foreign policy."

Bush's approach marks a departure, in many ways, from the policy of diplomatic engagement that former President Bill Clinton pursued with Russia, China and North Korea.

Clinton's critics charged that he went too far in trying to accommodate governments in those countries with policies that bordered on appeasement.

"If you start mollycoddling China, you run the risk of basically appeasing them," said former U.S. diplomat John Tkacik, president of China Business Intelligence, an Alexandria, Va., consulting firm. "Who knows what the Chinese will do?"

The Bush tack also carries risks, however, including the possibility of missing opportunities to make partners of former foes or a miscalculation that could spark countermeasures.

---

4. Article by Bob Deans from *The Atlanta Journal* March 25, 2001. Copyright © Cox News Service. Reprinted with permission.

Critics of the Bush approach even suggest that it threatens to undermine progress made during the past decade, as Russia has embarked on democratic and free-market reforms and China has worked to open its economy and much of its society to the outside world.

"The single greatest challenge of this early part of the 21st century is to integrate Russia and China into the international democratic and economic system," said Robert Pastor, political science professor at Emory University in Atlanta.

"A lot of the statements that (members of the Bush foreign policy team) are making to try to reflect a new toughness makes sense if your vision is a new Cold War," Pastor said. "But it sure doesn't help

---

"The single greatest challenge of this early part of the 21st century is to integrate Russia and China into the international democratic and economic system."—**Robert Pastor, Emory University**

---

you to facilitate (Russia's and China's) integration into a new world system. It just gets their backs up. It elicits from Russia and China the kind of negative and hostile activities that are really a thing of the past."

Bush has suggested he isn't spoiling to renew frictions between the United States and its Cold War rivals, with whom he hopes to cooperate on increased trade and in addressing global ills ranging from AIDS to terrorism.

"Nothing we do is a threat to you," Bush told Chinese Vice Premier Qian Qichen in an Oval Office meeting Thursday, striking a similar note the next day with respect to Russia.

"I believe we can have good, strong relations with the Russians," Bush said. "They'll just understand my administration is one that takes firm positions when we think we're right."

Some of what appears to be a shift in policy could be little more than a change in the rhetorical tone between Bush, who describes himself as something of a linguistic minimalist, and Clinton, who was ever ready to go on at length to lay out nuanced and specific foreign policy positions.

"People will find that I'm a straightforward person," Bush told Qian, "that I represent my country's interests in a very straightforward way."

In recent weeks, though, Bush has clearly toughened the edge on U.S. relations with China, Russia and North Korea.

Secretary of State Colin Powell expelled four Russian agents here on diplomatic passports, claiming each was "directly implicated" in the case of Robert Hanssen, the FBI agent arrested last month and charged with spying for the Russians.

Powell told Russian Ambassador Yuri Ushakov that other Russians would have to leave as well, in reductions that could ultimately affect dozens of Russian agents, the largest such expulsion since the Reagan presidency.

The action didn't go down well in Moscow.

Russia expelled four American diplomats in a retaliatory move, and Foreign Minister Igor Ivanov called the U.S. measure "a hostile act, aimed at increasing tension in Russian-American relations." Ivanov warned that "those trying to push mankind and the United States toward the Cold War and confrontation will fail."

U.S.-China relations have been tested, as well, as the Pentagon considers whether to sell advanced Aegis radar defense equipment next month to Taiwan, which Beijing regards as a renegade province.

And, in his meeting with Qian, Bush openly criticized China's record on human rights and religious repression.

Next door to China on the Korean Peninsula, Bush said earlier this month, he would largely abandon the Clinton approach of detente and diplomacy. That approach had produced a two-year moratorium on North Korea's missile development and production and had taken the two countries to the brink of an accord that might have ended a half-century of enmity between the Cold War foes.

Bush said the Clinton approach lacked verification. Powell said the Bush administration is reviewing the U.S. approach to North Korea, still a harshly repressive totalitarian state.

"We will do it in a measured way, with clear-eyed realism," Powell told the Senate Foreign Relations Committee, "and, at a time when we're ready and a time we're prepared to engage, we will then engage at that time."

Five Ways Bush Can Brighten Latin America's Mood[5]

BY PETER HAKIM
CHRISTIAN SCIENCE MONITOR, MARCH 28, 2001

The mood of Latin American leaders was downbeat in Chile last week at the Inter-American Development Bank's annual meeting. Argentina's economic and political turmoil was the main source of unease, but the U.S. economic slide and uncertainties about the Bush administration's foreign policy directions also contributed to the bad humor.

During the presidential campaign and after, George W. Bush gave the United States' southern neighbors reason to expect new and more constructive policy directions from Washington. Time and again, he has emphasized that U.S. interests would be served by more cooperative hemispheric relationships.

He has already visited Mexico and, by the time he travels to Quebec City on April 21 for a summit of Western Hemisphere heads of state, he will have met with half a dozen Latin American presidents. The summit, the third since 1994, will be the first public test of his commitment to building partnerships in the Americas.

President Bush faces five challenges:

- **Convince his Latin American and Caribbean counterparts of a U.S. commitment to establishing a Free Trade Area of the Americas.** Negotiations over the FTAA—which promises more secure access to U.S. markets and investment capital—have lagged badly because of the White House's failure to gain "fast track" trade negotiating authority from Congress. Since there's no time to win that authority by April 21, all President Bush can do is promise to move ahead promptly. If he does not take quick action, however, interest in the FTAA—and in broader cooperation with the U.S.—will wane.

- **Ease the concerns of Latin American leaders about U.S. policy toward Colombia, which is racked by guerrilla and criminal violence.** Most regional leaders are unhappy with the military emphasis of U.S. policy and want Washington to take seriously their concerns about the escalating violence and its spill-over into neighboring countries. Mr. Bush mainly has to listen attentively here. But the other presidents would welcome an announcement from him that the U.S. is now ready to accept the Colombian president's invitation to join the group of nations monitoring government-guerrilla peace talks. This would provide some measure of reassurance that Washington, in fact, supports a peaceful settlement.

- **Reinforce the collective defense of democracy in Latin America by joining the other leaders to consolidate advances in dealing with potentially violent national conflicts.** Specifically, they should give the Organization of American States a formal mediating role in resolving internal disputes that threaten peace or democracy. This is what the OAS did in Peru last year when it orchestrated a dialogue between the government and the country's opposition groups to establish ground rules for new elections. A similar effort has made halting progress in Haiti.

- **Strengthen U.S.-Latin American cooperation in fighting illicit drugs.** He can do so simply by endorsing—as a potential substitute for unilateral U.S. certification—the OAS's multilateral mechanism for assessing national antidrug campaigns in the hemisphere. In its first application, the OAS procedure turned out a set of highly professional evaluations. If the U.S. agrees, this could soon replace the U.S. process, which has produced more conflict and bitterness than coordination in hemispheric counter-narcotics efforts.

- **Improve education throughout the Americas.** Nothing is more important for Latin America's future, nor for the region's capacity to participate in a constructive partnership with the U.S. The discouraging recent performance of Latin America's economies reflects inferior education systems. The 1998 summit was called the "education summit" because the participating governments all made extensive commitments to school reform; little has been accomplished since then. With the priority he has assigned to domestic education goals, President Bush has the authority to call for every country to commit itself to education reform. This time, though, he should insist on clear performance criteria, procedures for measuring progress, and the allocation of sufficient resources to accomplish this task.

By pursuing these initiatives, President Bush can reinvigorate U.S. leadership in the hemisphere, and reassure his Latin American colleagues that the United States is, indeed, ready for partnership.

II. European Relations

Dritto   *Rovescio*

The Disney character Scrooge McDuck graces the front ("dritto") of a sample euro coin distributed to Italian school children, while the euro symbol is imprinted on the back ("rovescio"), with the words "United Europe" encircling the lower half of the coin.

Editor's Introduction

Relations with Europe have remained extremely vital to U.S. interests since the end of World War II. It was then that the Soviet Union pushed westward, acquiring Eastern European countries such as Yugoslavia, Poland, and Romania. Western Europe had been ravaged by World War II and was not strong enough to prevent further Soviet expansion. In light of these circumstances, British prime minister Winston Churchill enlisted American support in a speech where he warned that "an iron curtain has descended across the [European] continent," dividing East from West. The United States, with its huge nuclear arsenal, would protect Western Europe during the subsequent forty years of cold war.

The European nation in which the cold war was played out most dramatically was Germany. The Berlin Wall, erected in 1961, split that city in two and was a physical reminder of the ideological and cultural division between the Soviet Union and the Western world. While the eastern half of Germany was ruled by a Soviet-backed communist government, installed after World War II, the western half became a democratic republic with a strong economy. After the fall of the Berlin Wall in 1989, two years before the Soviet collapse, Germany reunited and, despite the burden of rehabilitating the Eastern zone, remains the dominant economic power in Europe. When the Eastern European states broke away from communist control, they sought both military and economic alliances with the West.

Europe has begun the process of uniting by creating a European Union with a single currency, the Euro. Europeans have newfound pride, and though they remain America's strongest allies, they often resent the U.S. military presence on the continent now that the threat of Soviet invasion has subsided. President George W. Bush's plan for a missile defense system adds fuel to European protests against American displays of military might. It does not help that American businesses and pop culture already threaten to overwhelm Europe's own.

Henry Kissinger's article, "Troubling How U.S., Europe Falling Apart," discusses European disapproval of the U.S. economic sanctions on Cuba, Iran, and Iraq; of the proposed missile defense system that the U.S. would deploy partly to defend Europe; and of the American reliance on capital punishment at home. Kissinger nevertheless points out that emotional bonds between America and Europe have strengthened as more citizens—especially the newly freed East Europeans—visit one another's countries. The next article, a letter from former Soviet leader Mikhail Gorbachev to George W. Bush, "A

Blunt Plea, to Bush from Gorbachev," encourages the United States to use its vast power to help countries whose citizens live "in abject poverty, degradation, and backwardness." "Shifts in Europe Pose Prickly Challenge to U.S.," by Roger Cohen, concentrates on Europe's and America's roles in the North Atlantic Treaty Organization (N.A.T.O.). Cohen explains how the European Union wants to establish its own military apart from N.A.T.O. The final article in this section, "U.S. Leadership Is Compromised by Death Penalty," by Felix Rohatyn, questions America's use of capital punishment, which to Europeans seems barbarous. The debate is most passionate in France, where 500,000 citizens signed a petition against the death penalty and presented it to the U.S. Embassy in Paris.

Troubling How U.S., Europe Pulling Farther Apart[1]

By Henry Kissinger
Houston Chronicle, January 14, 2001

The uneasy reaction of European media and political leaders to the American election, ascribed to a desire for continuity, actually involved a remarkable paradox. Why continuity when Atlantic relations have been far from harmonious?

Our allies, Britain largely excepted, have been dissociating, often demonstratively, from sanctions against Cuba, Iran or Iraq, and from American policy on the Arab-Israeli conflict and in the Taiwan Straits. They have disagreed publicly with the concept of a national missile defense, which French President Jacques Chirac attacked at a press conference at the side of Russian President Vladimir Putin, explicitly on behalf of all of Europe. The European Union is in the process of creating a military force institutionally distinct from NATO. Since the end of the Cold War, common policy toward the Soviet Union has been replaced by allies seeking their own "special relationship" with Moscow—not necessarily directed against other allies but not especially solicitous of their views either.

The disagreements in the economic field are even more visible. The United States has threatened retaliation against Europe over bananas and beef, and the European Union has threatened the United States over American taxation of exports. The two sides are deadlocked on how, or even whether, to launch a new multilateral trade negotiation. Another dispute over energy policy looms, especially if oil prices remain high.

Equally striking is the weakening of the emotional bond. More Americans and Europeans are visiting each others' continents than ever before. But they travel in the cocoon of their preconceptions or of their professional relationships, without acquiring a knowledge of the history and politics of the other side. On the other hand, the United States, as depicted in European mass media, is defined by the death penalty, the lack of a system of free medical insurance, the vast American prison population and other comparable stereo-

---

1. Article by Henry Kissinger from *Houston Chronicle* January 14, 2001. Copyright © Henry Kissinger. Reprinted with permission.

types. In this atmosphere, many advocates of European integration are urging unity as an exercise in differentiation from, if not opposition to, the United States.

The Clinton administration has left a legacy of unanswered questions: Is the Atlantic alliance still at the heart of trans-Atlantic relations? If so, how does it define its purpose in the post–Cold War world? If not, what can be put in its place to undergird trans-Atlantic relations?

The paradox is that, the political vacuum notwithstanding, personal relations among the leaders of the Atlantic nations during the 1990s remained remarkably close. But they were based less on shared policy views than on shared personal experiences as the first group of leaders who had grown up after World War II. The founding generation of the alliance presumed the benevolence of American power and the importance of allied unity. Their sons and daughters, growing up during the protest movements of the 1960s and 1970s, developed a profound distrust of American power; at a minimum, they wanted America to use its power only for universal causes transcending the national interest.

The founding generation viewed the alliance as the point of departure for a union of democracies. The generation governing in the 1990s viewed the Atlantic alliance as a relic of the Cold War, if not an obstacle to overcoming it. Its goal was less to strengthen the alliance than to "erase dividing lines." Thus, in a joint press conference with Russian President Boris Yeltsin in March 1997, President Clinton described the "old NATO" as "basically a mirror image of the Warsaw Pact," equating a voluntary association of democracies with what the Soviet Union had imposed on subjugated countries.

The key to the paradox is that, throughout the West, foreign relations are today more than ever a function of domestic politics. Since the European center-left governments have disappointed the radical wings of their parties by implementing economic reform based on the market, they are reluctant to inflame these further by implementing national security policies identified with the United States. On the other hand, the domestic opposition to President Bill Clinton's foreign policy came generally from the right. Because of this difference in domestic politics, European leaders saw no contradiction between their personal admiration—and even affection—for Clinton and vocal opposition to policies they conceived as having been partly imposed on him.

So it happened that the most harmonious encounters of the European leaders with President Clinton occurred at "Third Way" get-togethers of world—mostly European—social democratic leaders. These are gatherings at which leaders of the center left have struggled to define a new agenda after having acquiesced in the Reagan-

Thatcher revolution in market economics. This is why the Socialist prime minister of Portugal was invited to these gatherings and the conservative prime minister of Spain was not; why the Socialist prime minister of France attended but the conservative president of France was excluded. In attending as a regular participant, Clinton threw the prestige of the American presidency behind one side in the domestic politics of the countries represented.

The advent of a Republican administration will inevitably change America's focus of consultation with Europe's leaders. They will be less geared to personalities and more designed to bring about

> **The Cold War has ended, but history and geography have not been abolished.**

a meaningful trans-Atlantic dialogue based on congruent, permanent national interests regardless of party. The previous record of service of the new national security team in Washington makes it very likely that the task of revitalizing the alliance will be given high priority.

Nostalgia for Cold War certitudes is no guide to a wise policy. But neither is the rote reiteration of slogans of Atlantic solidarity belied by the day-to-day conduct of foreign policy. The basic challenge is whether the Western democracies can rediscover a sense of common destiny. The Cold War has ended, but history and geography have not been abolished. Whether the Atlantic alliance can remain relevant to the new necessities depends on how it deals with issues of traditional security, how successful it is in promoting stability to the east of Europe and stability along Europe's southern frontier and in the Middle East.

The security issue presents itself as an insurance policy against a re-imperializing Russia, as missile defense and as the new European army (Euroforce).

A new trans-Atlantic dialogue on missile defense is urgently needed. European critics must ask themselves whether any American president can seriously be asked to leave his people permanently vulnerable to the threats generated by proliferating nuclear technology. American policy-makers need to find a way to show the relevance of their concerns and strategy to European necessities. Both sides have an obligation to re-examine a concept of deterrence that, if it fails, would produce tens of millions of casualties in a matter of hours.

As for the European army, the key issue is not whether Europe should have an autonomous voice but whether the Euroforce represents a diversion of resources, and what Europe means by autonomy. Specifically, how can the strategic objectives of the Euroforce be reconciled with the shrinking defense budgets in almost all the European countries? Even if existing budgets are maintained, the Euroforce would avoid a net diminution of allied defense only if it generated an overall increase of allied defense spending. And what, in practice, is the meaning of an autonomy according to which, in EU language, the Euroforce operates only where "NATO as a whole is not involved"?

An agreed division of labor is conceivable, though care must be taken not to suggest a degree of American dissociation that invites pressures from other countries. But what if the EU acts without the concurrence of the United States—that is, if, in effect, all members of the alliance except America and Canada go to war? Would, in such circumstances, the Euroforce have access to NATO logistics and intelligence that are in the main American? Would the United States come to the rescue if things went wrong?

Finally, would, at NATO meetings where the use of force is discussed, the Americans encounter colleagues who have already reached a collective EU decision, imposing procedures on NATO that are inconsistent with its entire history? European leaders who question missile defense because it might lead to the decoupling of American security from that of Europe should take care not to adopt institutions that drift inevitably toward political decoupling.

The key test is the ability to re-establish political coherence in trans-Atlantic relations. Absent that, the Euroforce could produce the worst of all worlds: disruption of NATO procedures and impairment of allied cooperation without enhanced allied military capability or meaningful European autonomy.

The trans-Atlantic relationship faces as well major geopolitical and economic challenges. To the east of NATO and the EU, the domestic arrangements that followed the demise of the Soviet Union are ending, if only because the generation that inherited power is passing from the scene. Chaos (or Russian domination) beckons unless the nations bordering the North Atlantic define it as a common problem and deal with it energetically as a common policy. It is particularly important to improve the coherence of efforts to bring Russia into the international community. Though every ally asserts that it serves the common cause, the definition of the common cause has, so far, remained elusive.

The future of the Mediterranean basin and the Middle East pose comparable challenges. There, the pressures of globalization and of demographic growth could usher in a period of adjustment and turmoil that makes the post-communist dislocations in the Balkans seem like child's play. Promoting stability in the Persian Gulf remains essential to allow both sides of the Atlantic access to reasonably priced energy.

Finally, the threat of economic recession brings home the need for cooperative measures by the nations representing well over half of the world's productive capacities. For Europe, this involves a demographic problem as well. In almost all European countries, the birth rate will not sustain even the present population, which is already inadequate to meet the demand for labor. The percentage of those having to be supported by a shrinking labor force will rise dramatically; the overall population of most European states will decline precipitously—adding to the pressures to expand immigration with all its political, social and cultural implications.

All these tasks could provide a rich agenda for a trans-Atlantic dialogue. Yet the European Union, by its procedures and much of its motivation, seeks to keep the United States at arm's length. When American officials encounter spokesmen for the supranational Europe, they discover that their interlocutors have very little flexibility because decisions already taken by the EU Council of Ministers (in which the United States does not participate even as an observer) can be altered only by going through the entire internal European process again. Traditional channels of U.S.-European cooperation are drying up with respect to economic matters. Analogous procedures are now being proposed as well for foreign and security policy. A balance must be found between the United States acting as if it were a member of European institutions, and being so marginalized as not to be able to participate in discussions affecting major American interests.

In short, what the alliance needs is not continuity so much as a sense of direction. Are the challenges described here growing pains of Europe's integration, or do they represent a conscious (or subconscious) European decision to forge a separate, competitive, future? On the answer to this question may depend the future of freedom and peace in a world without Cold War and seeking to wrest a global order out of turbulence.

Shifts in Europe Pose Prickly Challenge to U.S.[2]

BY ROGER COHEN
NEW YORK TIMES, FEBRUARY 11, 2001

A little phrase from Rudolf Scharping, the German defense minister, recently caused American military commanders to shudder: "As the European Union develops its security and defense policy and becomes an independent actor, we must determine our security policy with Russia, our biggest neighbor."

The specter of Europe—and particularly its central power, Germany—adopting a more independent stance from NATO and paying close heed to Russia is chilling for the United States, and hard to reconcile with the Atlantic alliance that has preserved Europe's stability and advanced American interests for more than a half-century.

The alliance is not about to fall apart: too much is at stake for that, not least the peace of mind of the many Europeans who still believe this continent is inherently unstable unless America is present. But as Mr. Scharping's words suggest, something fundamental has shifted in the transatlantic relationship.

The 15-member European Union, long a mere trade bloc ultimately protected by American power, has begun to develop into a grouping with its own serious military and strategic ambitions. Where exactly such ambitions are directed remains uncertain, but this much seems clear: the scope of Europe's quest for an altered balance of power in its post–Cold War ties with Washington is not yet fully appreciated by the Bush administration.

Addressing the allies for the first time last week in Munich, Defense Secretary Donald H. Rumsfeld did not use the words "European Union" once.

It was this omission—as much as Mr. Rumsfeld's stark warning to the Europeans to avoid "actions that could reduce NATO's effectiveness by confusing duplication or by perturbing the transatlantic link"—that was noted in European capitals.

"It appeared that the European Union was not yet on Mr. Rumsfeld's radar screen," said Wolfgang Ischinger, a senior official in the German Foreign Ministry. "Of course, it was not a factor the last

---

time he was in office. But the fact is the development of the Union's defense identity is an accelerating process that it would be a mistake to oppose."

Already, the European Union has set up a military planning staff, established a so-called political and security committee and is readying a 60,000-member rapid reaction force. At the same time, most of the Union is less than a year away from the fast-forward to a European identity likely to occur when the euro becomes the currency on the streets of Barcelona, Brussels and Berlin. The euro was always a political project; its politics involve forging a united Europe as a counterweight to American dominance.

How the Europeans finesse their challenge to American superpower assumptions has yet to be defined. France, for example, wants Europe's new military arm to be "independent" from NATO, or at least equipped to be so; Britain rejects such ideas as destabilizing Gallic dreams. But Europe has clearly decided to create the embryo of an army because it has determined that this is in its interest, because it believes that this is the only way to convince skeptical electorates of the need to increase defense spending, and because it views the development as an essential complement to economic and political integration.

It wants to be treated as a bloc and as an equal within the alliance, so ending the relationship of a single superpower to a bunch of far smaller allies. For Joschka Fischer, the German foreign minister, such European integration amounts to a "historical process" and, as such, is unstoppable—even by America.

The parallels are obvious to another development portrayed as unstoppable and inevitable by President Bush: the American construction and deployment of a system of national missile defense of which Europeans remain suspicious.

As these two projects—Europe's rapid reaction force, America's missile shield—confront each other, a profound change in transatlantic relations seems clear. At other times of post-war tensions, like the resistance in Germany, Italy, Britain and elsewhere to the deployment of new medium-range missiles in the early 1980's, the arguments centered on a European reaction to an American-directed policy.

This time, however, both Europe and the United States are pushing ideas they perceive to be in their inviolable interests. Neither is ready to budge. Each will have to accommodate the other. In this sense, the European Union has become an "actor"—unwieldy, underfunded—but still a body that acts as well as reacts.

Across the broad range of European-American differences—from subsidies for the new Airbus "Superjumbo" aircraft to what diplomats now call the "social conflicts" over issues like gun control, the death penalty and the use of genetically modified food—this growing European coherence weighs heavily.

The issues may prove especially intractable because, as Mr. Ischinger noted, "We now have a different thinking about power and structures."

Europeans have just traded in a lot of their national sovereignty for the euro and so view the world very much in multilateral terms. The United States remains fiercely attached to its sovereignty; the new administration wants to bolster national defense as it questions automatic recourse to multilateralism.

"Europe must not become a middle ground between NATO on the one hand and Russia on the other."—Gen. Wesley K. Clark, former NATO commander in Europe

---

As at any time of strategic flux, there seem to be real dangers of misunderstanding. "Increased European capabilities are a political imperative for both sides of the Atlantic," said Gen. Wesley K. Clark, the former NATO commander in Europe who retired recently. "But the evolution of European capabilities should not distance the European Union from NATO. Europe must not become a middle ground between NATO on the one hand and Russia on the other."

A lot of thinking has already gone into ensuring this does not happen. NATO and the European Union are going to meet at ambassadorial level six times a year and at ministerial level at least once a year to ensure that, to use Mr. Rumsfeld's phrase, Europe's new defense plans do not end up "injecting instability" into the alliance. These meetings will involve bizarre overlapping—11 of NATO's 19 members are also members of the European Union—but reflect a determination to avoid misunderstandings. Still, many American questions remain.

What missions exactly is the new European force to serve? When, if ever, would Europe want to act militarily without the United States? Will scarce resources not be diverted from NATO? Is duplication not inevitable?

American officials also ask whether it would not be better to increase defense spending—a mere 1.4 percent of gross national product in Germany compared to about 3.5 percent in the United

States—rather than paying for new institutions. And they wonder why Congress should approve funding for NATO if Europe has its own defense structure.

"The danger is that the Europeans will set up the European Union as a competitor and alternative to NATO," said one American military expert. "Then they say to the Russians, 'Don't worry, work with us, we know the United States is too forceful.' At that point, different geography and different interests become impossible to contain within NATO."

The Europeans dismiss such concerns. They point to the fact that the United States—most recently in the Balkans—has repeatedly called on Europe to become more capable of projecting force and acting coherently. They recall the Kosovo war, where the European

---

> **"The danger is that the Europeans will set up the European Union as a competitor and alternative to NATO."**—an American military expert

---

contribution was compromised by the continent's technological arrears. They say a strong alliance for the 21st century must be a balanced one.

At present, there are only about 50 centralized European military planning staff—compared to more than eight times that at NATO military headquarters. Britain, backed by Germany, argues for planning to remain essentially under NATO's control.

But France wants Europe to have a large and independent military planning staff. Meanwhile, Turkey—an alliance member angered at being excluded from the nascent European forces—has balked at allowing NATO to plan for the Europeans.

In the end, however, it seems clear that Europe needs America—for the practical military reason that only America has the airlift, reconnaissance and intelligence equipment to make a mission feasible, and for the strategic reason that in a Europe where America is no longer a power, German power becomes uncomfortably conspicuous.

And Mr. Bush may find that he needs the Europeans for his national missile defense system—for the practical reason that a deep transatlantic rift would be very costly in trade and other areas, and strategically to preserve alliances.

For now, the Europeans seem ready to adopt a wait-and-see approach to Mr. Bush's idea. Their resistance is real and their concerns serious: what if, for example, China increases its missile force, exports missiles and thus goads India into following suit?

Mr. Bush's plan now seems to be part of a general military reassessment that could involve large unilateral cuts in the American nuclear arsenal. As such, it is certain to be more palatable to the Europeans.

"On missile defense, we have decided on a soft approach combined with pressing questions," said Mr. Ischinger. "But the Americans must understand that no real military threats are perceived by most Germans and there is no way we can sell a larger defense budget unless we push forward the creation of a European force."

Such "understanding" still has to be reached in Washington. "Weaken NATO and we weaken Europe, which weakens all of us," Mr. Rumsfeld said in Munich, at the gathering where Mr. Scharping alarmed Americans with his glimpse of other defense options. The fact is that a stronger, more united, less vulnerable Europe, with no enemy at its door, no longer sees its interests in such straightforward terms.

One senior NATO official likened the adjustments now needed in the alliance as a result of Europe's growing cohesion and ambitions to "brain surgery—important, essential, doable, but if it goes wrong, a disaster."

U.S. Leadership Is Compromised by Death Penalty[3]

By Felix G. Rohatyn
Newsday, February 21, 2001

A subject rarely noted today is the challenge to America's moral leadership in Europe. Most Frenchmen, as most Europeans, admire America. They admire what we do, what we stand for and what we have done for them twice in the 20th Century. I have had the privilege of speaking on D-Day at the Normandy military cemeteries and seeing tens of thousands of Frenchmen paying their respects to the fallen GIs. France considers itself, together with the United States, as the source of human rights and modern democracy.

It is important for the United States to maintain this image in the eyes of Europeans and to protect the legitimacy of our moral leadership. This moral leadership is under challenge because of two issues: the death penalty and violence in our society.

During my nearly four years in France, no single issue evoked as much passion and as much protest as executions in the United States. Repeated protests in front of the embassy in Paris, protests at our consulates and, just recently, a petition signed by 500,000 French men and women delivered to our embassy in Paris were part of a constant refrain. My colleague in Germany, Ambassador John Kornblum, had indicated to me that he was challenged as frequently in Germany on this issue as I was in France.

In France, the death penalty was outlawed in 1981, even though it was still favored by a majority. The European Union outlaws the death penalty. There is a strong belief among our European allies that it has no place in a civilized society.

In addition, the United States is seen as executing people who have not had appropriate legal assistance, people who may be innocent, people who are mentally retarded as well as minors. We are viewed as executing disproportionate numbers of minorities and poor people, and there is no compelling statistical evidence that the death penalty is a greater deterrent to potential criminals than other forms of punishment.

---

3. Article by Felix Rohatyn from *Newsday* February 21, 2001. Copyright © Felix Rohatyn. Reprinted with permission.

When Gov. George H. Ryan of Illinois, a Republican who supported the death penalty, announced a moratorium on executions in his state, I decided I had to rethink the issue as well as be willing to address it in interviews and questions that followed my every public appearance.

As a New Yorker who had lived in a high-crime environment, I had always been favorable to the death penalty, at least for certain major crimes. As chairman of New York's Municipal Assistance Corp., I had worked with two governors, Mario Cuomo and Hugh Carey, who regularly vetoed the penalty, but it was Ryan's moratorium, together with repeated reports about incompetent legal representation, that made me take this issue more seriously.

> *This is a hard issue, but crime and punishment are hard issues.*

And it was sustained exposure to this issue in Europe, in interviews, in Q&As at universities or just in social encounters, that brought me around to supporting a moratorium while we review the whole issue of capital punishment.

I certainly do not believe that, just because our allies oppose the death penalty, we should automatically follow. After all, the French legal system has its own shortcomings. France does not provide for "habeas corpus," which I find incomprehensible in a democratic society, and French jails are in dismal condition, according to a French study published recently.

But I believe that the reality of the situation is that neither we nor our European allies can be proud of our criminal justice systems. The Europeans have a mandatory release system that returns the most odious criminals to the street after a maximum of 20 to 30 years, which I could not support, while we sometimes execute the wrong people and turn our jails into graduate schools for crime, which is no better.

This is a hard issue, but crime and punishment are hard issues. The Constitution speaks of "cruel and unusual punishment." Some 300 million of our closest allies think capital punishment is cruel and unusual. It might be worthwhile to give it some further thought. I was able to have a rational dialogue on this issue in France by suggesting that neither we nor Europe had found an appropriate answer to the challenges of crime and punishment, to the reform of the penal system as a whole and to the challenge of rehabilitation together with the necessity for appropriate punishment.

The death penalty, guns, violence in society—these cast a large cloud on America's moral leadership. I believe it would be worth having a dialogue on these difficult subjects with our Atlantic allies—not by diplomats but by jurists and parliamentarians and chiefs of police. At a time when our military, economic and political power, our so-called "hegemony," is a source of concern to many of our allies, it is important that our moral leadership be sustained.

III. Military Intervention

Alexander Zemlianichenko/AP Photo

American and Russian soldiers, members of a multinational peace force, stand side by side at Tuzla Airbase in Bosnia on February 7, 1996.

Editor's Introduction

Since the end of the Cold War, the United States has engaged in military operations throughout the world, primarily through N.A.T.O. and the United Nations. Because of its advanced military technology and superior force, the U.S. has led these missions but has faced objections from its close European and Asian allies for doing so. Along with the political costs of being the world's lone superpower have come more personal ones, such as the 148 American lives lost in the Persian Gulf War, though that figure pales in comparison with the tens of thousands of Iraqis who died in the conflict. Since the Gulf War, the United States has led other military operations in the Balkans and Somalia, each of which has resulted in a limited losses to allied forces but has largely failed in its mission to end hostilities in those regions.

"Sheathing the Big Stick," by James Kitfield discusses President Saddam Hussein's defiance of the United Nations' weapons inspection teams in the years since the Gulf War. Kitfield examines the effectiveness of the standing threat of U.S. force if Iraq fails to comply with the United Nations Special Commission on Iraq (U.N.S.C.O.M.), which regulates Iraq's arsenal of nuclear weapons. While the U.S. is better equipped than other nations to enact such reprisals on "rogue states" like Iraq, maintaining the strongest military is very expensive. The price tags of the latest F-22s and F/A-18E/F Super Hornet, for example, are astounding. Given the tremendous financial outlay involved, James Thurman's "The Costs and Benefits of Ruling the Skies" raises the question, "How modern does the U.S. military need to be?"

In 1983 President Ronald Reagan proposed building a space-based missile defense shield that would destroy incoming nuclear warheads. George W. Bush now wants to resurrect this program—popularly called "Star Wars"—on a smaller scale, with a ground- or sea-based shield, rather than one that is space-based. "Moving Target" is Carla Robbins's report on the president's argument for building this system, which he claims will enable us to "defend against the new threats of the 21st century." One of those threats is posed by China, according to a C.I.A. report outlining scenarios for a new arms race with that nation. While he has been forced into particular vigilance about this threat since the spy plane incident of March 2001, President Bush believes that the proposed missile shield will provide adequate protection against threats from hostile nations and terrorist groups. On this ground he plans to decrease American military operations, as David Sanger reports in "A New View of Where America Fits in the World," and pursue a "more humble foreign policy" with less involvement abroad.

Defense: Sheathing the Big Stick[1]

By James Kitfield
National Journal, August 22, 1998

Earlier this month, by defying U.N. weapons inspectors yet again, Saddam Hussein threw into sharp relief a big shift in U.S. policy toward the Iraqi dictator. Not only did Secretary of State Madeleine K. Albright avoid the customary threats of military force to back up U.N. inspections but—as first reported by *The Washington Post* on Aug. 14—she went so far as to persuade chief weapons inspector Richard Butler, executive chairman of the U.N. Special Commission (UNSCOM), to drop plans for surprise searches that might have rapidly escalated the confrontation.

The genesis for that shift in policy came last February, when it appeared to all the world that Saddam Hussein blinked in a showdown with U.S. military forces. Faced with imminent strikes by an armada of American aircraft and warships, Saddam agreed to an 11th-hour deal brokered by U.N. Secretary General Kofi Annan to let U.N. inspectors search once again for weapons of mass destruction. But in truth, Clinton administration officials felt profoundly troubled by events surrounding the February face-off.

In fact, after a thorough policy review of that crisis, U.S. officials concluded that Saddam Hussein's rope-a-dope strategy—periodically forcing a showdown with American military forces over U.N. inspections—was widening fissures in the U.N. Security Council and undermining international support for continued economic sanctions on Iraq.

The administration was also startled by the apparent lack of domestic support for military action: Opinion polls in February showed a majority of Americans favoring a diplomatic solution over a limited military action that would doubtless leave Saddam Hussein in power. Seven years of Iraqi provocations and crisis deployments are also straining U.S. military forces already stretched thin around the globe.

Publicly, administration officials have taken pains to play down how much their Iraqi policy has shifted. "We have ruled nothing out, including the use of force," Albright wrote in *The New York Times* on Aug. 17. "This is a confrontation between Iraq and the United Nations. It's up to Mr. Annan and the Security Council to make sure

---

that Saddam reverses course and cooperates with UNSCOM. And if they fail to persuade him to back down, we will have laid the foundation for our own decisive action."

Privately, administration officials concede that the downsides of using military force have persuaded them to wave a big stick only as a last resort instead of as a rote response to Iraqi provocations. "There's no doubt that as a result of the February showdown, we changed our tactics and are holding off on the threat of using military force—without giving up that option," said a knowledgeable White House source. "We'd be fools if we didn't learn over the years that Saddam Hussein had come to rely on our automatically threatening him militarily, to shift the debate from what he was doing to what we might do. Too often, the United States became the issue. So we learned that lesson well, and we're not going down that road."

The administration's growing reluctance to back the U.N. resolutions with American military might has raised a question, though: Is Washington's venerable strategy of keeping Iraq in its place by combining intrusive inspections for weapons with strict economic sanctions still viable? The increasing discontent with sanctions among Security Council members—especially Russia, China and France—and among Washington's Arab allies has already prompted many foreign policy experts to conclude that the present policy can't be sustained.

In the view of some experts, the United States should go one of two ways: either rely on passive deterrence of Iraq or officially target Saddam Hussein for overthrow. The recent shift in administration policy promises to reignite that debate over which strategy to pursue.

Michael Eisenstadt, a senior fellow at the Washington Institute for Near East Policy, said he sees "practical implications to this new policy that I'm afraid will exacerbate a bad situation. . . . In truth, Saddam has permitted access to UNSCOM weapons inspectors only under duress and the threat of military force. That meant he was constantly testing us. The bottom line, however, is that our perceived unwillingness to use force probably means that UNSCOM and the inspections regime cannot survive."

Sen. John McCain, R-Ariz., a member of the Armed Services Committee, criticizes what he sees as the administration's weakened resolve to eliminate the threat posed by Saddam Hussein. "We should never have consigned to Kofi Annan the responsibility for conducting U.S. policy towards Iraq, and I predicted at the time that Saddam would provoke another crisis, sooner rather than later. The administration just kicked the can down the road a ways," McCain said in an interview. "The question now is whether the administration will react to Saddam in a forceful way, including the threat of military action, or rather try to finesse the issue again. If they do the latter, the administration will raise profound suspicions that the rationale for our inaction is the president's domestic problems and his inability to rally the American people."

A Paucity of Options

Pleas for an immediate return to big-stick diplomacy against Saddam Hussein may be easy to deliver, but they could be underestimating the unpleasant realities. Some of the strongest voices urging a change in the policy that has permitted Saddam Hussein to provoke the U.S. military into action whenever he liked have come out of the Pentagon. According to high-placed sources, senior military leaders have been quietly, but forcefully, lobbying the White House to alter its Iraqi strategy. The most recent crisis alone—the latest in a string requiring the movement of substantial military forces to the Persian Gulf—cost the Defense Department $1.4 billion.

> *The most recent [Persian Gulf] crisis alone . . . cost the Defense Department $1.4 billion.*

"I don't think the American public really understands how terribly disruptive and expensive it is to move major military forces back and forth to the Persian Gulf," said retired Lt. Gen. James Terry Scott, director of the national security program at Harvard University's John F. Kennedy School of Government. Because the Pentagon can't budget for such sudden expenses, the money is initially taken from the military services' operations and maintenance accounts that pay for training troops and repairing equipment.

Another factor makes it harder for Washington to use military force against Iraq: the growing opposition to such a step among friendly Arab governments. "Many governments in the Persian Gulf region are suffering a severe backlash from the breakdown of the Arab-Israeli peace process, and Saddam has won the local public relations battle by constantly broadcasting the image of starving Iraqis," said Anthony Cordesman, a Middle East expert with the Center for Strategic and International Studies.

That's in addition to the evident desire by Russia, China and France to bring an early end to the U.N. economic sanctions so they can start trading again with Iraq. "If the United States had a more comprehensive strategy, and had avoided souring relations with Russia by expanding NATO and with the United Nations by refusing to pay our dues, we might have more leverage to line up support on the Security Council for a tough line against Iraq," said Richard Betts, director of the Institute for War and Peace Studies at Columbia University.

Administration officials insist that they can take unilateral military action against Iraq if Saddam continues to defy U.N. resolutions. But they're clearly concerned that doing so might bring an end to economic sanctions that have denied Iraq some $45 billion in oil revenue. Indeed, the shift in administration policy evident in recent weeks may well indicate a Faustian bargain—of sacrificing effective weapons inspections in order to keep economic sanctions in place.

"While weapons inspections and economic sanctions create a synergistic effect," the White House official said, "the sanctions are what prevents Saddam from rebuilding his military and weapons program. Maintaining sanctions is thus absolutely essential and central to our policy. For that reason, we don't want to be goaded into an ill-considered military response that would undercut support on the Security Council for continued sanctions and perhaps hasten the day when some countries might break with economic sanctions."

But essentially abandoning the threat of military force to back weapons inspections would dilute a key element of Washington's anti-Iraq containment policy and very likely renew calls for a bolder and riskier strategy to oust Saddam from power. An open letter to Clinton circulated earlier this year by former Rep. Stephen J. Solarz, D-N.Y., and former Reagan defense official Richard N. Perle—and signed by 40 former government officials and outside experts—does just that. It argues for providing financial aid and arms to Iraqi opposition groups and for arranging safe havens inside of Iraq protected by U.S. air cover.

"Everything we've learned about Saddam Hussein indicates that he is unrepentant and that, left to his own devices, he will rebuild his arsenal of weapons of mass destruction to intimidate his neighbors and reap vengeance on the United States," Solarz said in an interview. "Thus, the only solution is to get rid of Saddam."

The next few weeks and months will make plain whether the administration has simply adjusted its tactics in the lethal cat-and-mouse game with Saddam Hussein or has significantly altered its containment policy by withdrawing the threat of military force to back up U.N. resolutions.

"If the administration's tactic is designed to win broader support on the Security Council for forceful action should Saddam fail to back down, that strategy makes a lot of sense," Solarz said. "On the other hand, if this is a strategy for avoiding confrontation with Iraq, then the policy is sadly mistaken."

The Costs and Benefits of Ruling the Skies[2]

By James N. Thurman
Christian Science Monitor, August 4, 1999

One is intended to be a broom, sweeping skies clear of enemy aircraft. Another is a hammer, pounding hostile troops on the ground. The third is a decathlete, landing and taking off almost anywhere.

But does the U.S. need all three?

That's the question lawmakers on Capitol Hill are asking as they consider funding for three jet fighters—a decision that will help shape the direction of the U.S. military in the 21st century.

To the Pentagon, each aircraft performs a unique function—and thus all three are needed to help the U.S. maintain air superiority for the next 50 years.

But critics counter with one monolithic figure: $340 billion—the estimated cost of the three fighters over the next 20 years and the equivalent of the annual GDP of Russia.

The price tag is high enough that even many pro-defense members of Congress are balking. This clash over weaponry will affect all branches of the military. It also raises a question that is becoming increasingly pointed in the post Cold War: How modern does the U.S. military need to be?

"They have these three fighters on the books because they all evolved separately," says Ivan Eland, a defense expert at the Cato Institute here. "The question now is what do you do with them?"

The best known of the three new planes is the Air Force's F-22. Then there's the futuristic-looking Joint Strike Fighter (JSF) under development for all of the services but the Army. Incomplete prototypes of both are undergoing limited testing.

The third system, the Navy's F/A-18 E/F Super Hornet program, is far more evolved, with production under way.

The House recently axed $1.9 billion dollars for production of six F-22's, allocating $1.2 billion dollars for continued research and development. The Senate previously fully funded the program. Conferees are expected to restore at least some of the production money.

The $70 billion Raptor program was conceived during the Reagan years when the Cold War still ruled. Currently, in the midst of a new reality, $20 billion has been spent on research and development alone.

Lawmakers are questioning whether production costs will exceed the spending caps imposed by Congress. Lockheed-Martin, the principal contractor, says that won't happen. But skepticism remains in Congress that the platinum costs will go even higher.

Assurances against cost overruns are being made "by the people who originally told us these airplanes would cost $35 million a piece," says Rep. Jerry Lewis (R) of California, who led the effort to scrub production money for the plane in the House.

> *All the technological wizardry comes at a perhaps prohibitive cost.*

Pentagon strategists argue all that three are needed because each system is designed with separate battlefield functions.

With supersonic speeds, radar-evading stealth skin, and intercept capability, the F-22 is intended to create air dominance by shooting down enemy planes and eliminating radar and weapons sites.

The JSF is a multi-role fighter. "It is meant to attack targets on the ground but not meant to be a top-line dogfighter," says Michael O'Hanlon at the Brookings Institution in Washington.

Lockheed-Martin Corp. and the Boeing Company are competing to manufacture the JSF. With a potential order of as many as 3,000 aircraft, the Pentagon expects savings with mass production, paying between $28 and $36 million each.

The goal is to tailor the JSF to the needs of three services:

- The Air Force's version will replace the A-10 and F-16, delivering precision munitions with air-to-air combat capability.

- The Navy wants its stealth fighter-bomber version to be lighter than the Air Force's for carrier landings, but tough enough to take landings and take-offs at sea.

- The Marines want jump-jet ability, to get in and out of short runways.

The third major fighter system is the Navy's multi-role F/A-18 E/F Super Hornet. The carrier-based fighter carries nine tons of ordinance. It has expanded fuel capacity and size, extending its range.

But all the technological wizardry comes at a perhaps prohibitive cost. The JSF and F-22 would go into heavy production 10 to 15 years from now. That makes the fighter-jets a long term fiscal worry. It also ignores the present budget squeeze caused by escalating maintenance and production costs on the current fleet of fighters.

Upkeep of existing aircraft is already to the point that one of the five B-1B's deployed to Kosovo was sent "only as a source for spare parts," says Representative Lewis.

"The reason we are in a death spiral is we cannot choose," says Franklin Spinney, a program evaluator for the Department of Defense. "If I were God, I'd kill all three programs. We'd start over."

The Air Force vehemently defends the most expensive of the programs, the F-22. It argues that without the F-22, new versions of the SAM missile, as well as the advanced Eurofighter and the Russian SU35, will put the U.S. fleet at risk.

"The cost is affordable but I think you can see the value of the program is priceless," says Lt. Gen. Gregory Martin, an Air Force acquisition officer. He predicts the plane could dramatically reduce U.S. casualties in future conflicts.

But many of the F-22's gee-whiz features are untested, exacerbating concerns.

"Let's let the technology mature and do it right," says Chris Hellman, an analyst at the Center for Defense Information. "The thing is being rushed into production with a minimum of testing, which might be justified in the Cold War. But there is no legitimate reason to rush this thing."

Critics also say there are cheaper alternatives than the three jets, such as precision munitions and unmanned drone aircraft.

Rethinking the Next War[3]

BY MORTIMER B. ZUCKERMAN
U.S. NEWS & WORLD REPORT, MARCH 5, 2001

The world is in awe of the American war machine. Our Navy possesses a dozen immense supercarrier battle groups and dominates the seas; our nuclear submarines patrol the waters below; our fighters and bombers control the skies, supported by aerial tankers that allow them to fly half a world away and back. We alone have a worldwide satellite network providing constant intelligence and surveillance. Our Army possesses the world's best weapons, along with the best-trained and best-educated troops. Our smart weapons can cover hundreds of miles and hit a target within 1 meter. Our sea- and ground-launched ballistic missiles provide an overwhelming strategic deterrence. The cost is high. We spend more than the combined total of the next seven military powers. Our R&D budget alone, some $34 billion last year, exceeds the individual defense budgets of nearly all our NATO allies.

So why do we have to contemplate spending hundreds of billions more dollars? The answer is in the epigram from the trenches of World War I—that generals are always ready to fight the last war. America is all too ready to fight wars like the Gulf War—ready, in fact, to fight two such wars at once. But that is not the primary menace we face in the future. The need now is to cope with unconventional threats—so-called asymmetrical threats, which we cannot expect to fight from large, fixed bases. We must plan for longer-range warfare in which our forces will be dispersed and mobility will be at a premium. In Kosovo, for instance, the Army literally could not assemble its helicopter forces in time, and its tanks were too heavy to move over local roads and bridges. We will fight future battles from long distances using remote stand-off weapons that do almost everything that ground armor once did but with more flexibility, greater stealth, and less logistical support. This strategy acknowledges a limitation on our war machine—that we are more casualty-shy than the authoritarian societies we are likely to confront. Paradoxically, our overwhelming military power has made it clear to potential adversaries that their only hope is to offset it through some asymmetrical attack.

Taking stock. Our real dangers won't lie so much in the kind of hot TV scenes depicted in Kosovo, Bosnia, Haiti, Rwanda, or East Timor. They will lie in the proliferation of weapons of mass destruction, the possibility that Russia will lose control of its nuclear, chemical, and biological weapons, and that new forces of terrorism may threaten the United States at home, especially our vulnerable information systems. That is why Secretary of Defense Donald Rumsfeld wants a top-to-bottom strategic review.

The Clinton administration was reluctant to second-guess uniformed experts. But Rumsfeld, backed by President Bush and Vice President Cheney, has the expertise and confidence to address the key defense questions. For example: Do we need to station as many troops around the world? Do we need as many nuclear weapons on full alert? Does a two-major-theater war strategy have any relevance, given the 10-year decline of both Iraq and North Korea? Budgetary shares among the services have been relatively static to avoid strife within the Pentagon, but is that realistic? Do we need a separate agency to handle information systems, as well as recruitment and training of specialized personnel? Can we identify and eliminate redundant bases and expensive weaponry that the pork-barrel Congress foisted on the Pentagon? In sum, what structure, forces, and weapons do we need to carry out our strategy?

> *Our real dangers . . . will lie in the proliferation of weapons of mass destruction.*

Rumsfeld has wisely selected Andy Marshall to head this new review. He is a 27-year Pentagon veteran and acclaimed military analyst described by the *Economist* as "one of the most original military thinkers in America."

There is an interesting parallel in all this with the building of our transcontinental railway in the middle of the 19th century. We needed a military presence on the Plains and in the Rockies to protect the settlers heading west. The military had spent millions of dollars building forts, but without much effect on Indian attacks against settlers because the cavalry could not get to the fighting in time. Railroads made the difference. They gave the Army the ability to move troops faster and safer from one place to another, making the military more effective with fewer men and fewer forts. The lesson of the Plains stands today. By exploiting the latest technology, we can transform our military strategy and our military forces—and reduce our military costs.

Moving Target[4]

By Carla Anne Robbins
Wall Street Journal, February 9, 2001

President Bush is committed to building a national missile-defense system. What he has yet to explain is whose missiles, exactly, it would be defending against.

The potential threat could be a small number of missiles being sought by North Korea, Iraq and Iran. Or it could be a far-better-armed Russia gone bad, or a China bent on regional domination.

The decision about whom to defend against will play a big role in determining how ambitious and expensive a system is built. But even more is at stake. Mr. Bush's choice will help define America's post–Cold War enemies and shape America's place in the world for years to come.

Put bluntly, Mr. Bush will have to decide if he wants a system he can share with Russia and China, or one that he could someday use against them. The choice will determine whether the U.S. has much hope of winning the support of its European allies and the tolerance of Moscow and Beijing in this new world of missile defense, or whether it will have to go it alone.

It's a lot of uncertainty for a system whose costs are so high. Even the limited land-based system proposed by President Clinton was expected to cost at least $60 billion. If Mr. Bush decides to "layer" his defenses—combining ground, sea and even space-based systems—the price tag would go far higher.

As the president begins focusing on national-security issues next week, he will see a world very different from 1983, when Ronald Reagan proposed a space shield that could repel thousands of Soviet warheads. But the past decade's extraordinary changes have only confirmed for Mr. Bush and his supporters a belief that missile defenses are essential to long-term security. In a campaign that was light on foreign-policy debate, Mr. Bush devoted an entire speech last spring to a post–Cold War nuclear policy with a missile-defense system at its core "to defend against the new threats of the 21st century." On the stage with him was nearly every icon of the GOP foreign-policy establishment.

---

4. Reprinted from *The Wall Street Journal*. Copyright © 2001, Dow Jones & Company, Inc. All rights reserved.

Mr. Bush has sent contradictory messages about which countries pose those 21st-century threats. In his spring speech, he said the system would defend against "missile attacks by rogue nations or accidental launches." He has gone out of his way to reassure China and Russia that his system wouldn't have the power to deflect their arsenals. But in a September 1999 speech at the Citadel, considered his keynote defense-policy address, Mr. Bush had placed China squarely on the list of nations posing a threat to the U.S., along with

---

"In 1996, after some tension over Taiwan, a Chinese general reminded America that China possesses the means to incinerate Los Angeles with nuclear missiles."—
George W. Bush

North Korea, Iraq and Iran. "In 1996, after some tension over Taiwan, a Chinese general reminded America that China possesses the means to incinerate Los Angeles with nuclear missiles," he said.

Further muddying the mix is the question of who is to be protected. Mr. Bush has said that America's allies must also be covered—and hinted at bringing even the Russians under the umbrella.

At least some of the confusion has to do with the uncertainty about what the technology can do and would cost. The Reagan and Bush administrations spent $27 billion researching a host of exotic ideas, from orbiting warhead-zapping lasers to satellites with pop-up missile interceptors. Mr. Clinton was never a believer, though, and the only serious work in the past eight years was on a modest system of rocket interceptors based on land. With no other national missile-defense programs in development, predicting costs of other systems is next to impossible.

The confusion also stems from ideological splits within the GOP. There is fierce debate over whether to try to persuade Russia to amend the 1972 Anti-Ballistic Missile Treaty—which bans national missile defenses—and accept certain limits on what the U.S. builds, or to simply jettison the treaty as a Soviet-era relic and proceed.

Hints of such a fault line are already evident within the new national-security team. Defense Secretary Donald Rumsfeld dismissed the ABM treaty as "ancient history" and a "straitjacket" during his confirmation hearings. "I mean, to try to fashion something that fits within the constraints of that and expect that you're going to get the most effective program, the earliest to deploy and the most cost-effective—it boggles the mind," he said. A week later, Secretary of State Colin Powell, reflecting either his role as the country's top diplomat or a skepticism about missile defenses, told his own hearing that the treaty is "probably no longer relevant" but that there would be "a long way to go" and "a lot of conversations" with the Russians before the U.S. would walk away.

Mr. Bush also must decide how far he is willing to go to calm China's fears. While business interests in his party want to engage rather than confront Beijing, some missile-defense backers see China as the prime country to defend against. "For the sake of potential profits, many are quick to dismiss the rhetoric from Beijing as empty threats," Arizona GOP Sen. Jon Kyl warned in a *Washington Times* opinion piece. "What if China's leaders mean what they say?"

Most European leaders believe the threat of massive retaliation is enough to restrain the rogue states, so a missile defense isn't needed. And they fear that such a defense could spark a crisis with Moscow and Beijing and unravel all efforts at arms control. Such a move "cannot fail to relaunch the arms race in the world," French President Jacques Chirac said last week. Mr. Bush's campaign pledge to protect the allies hasn't improved attitudes.

Mr. Bush will first have to decide whether to continue with Mr. Clinton's plans for two sites of 250 ground-based interceptors designed to seek out and smash into incoming warheads as they hurtle through space. For the former president, who embraced missile defense only under political duress, the rogue states were the only targets, and what the system couldn't do was as important as what it could. "We put on the table a system that objectively posed no threat to Russia's strategic arsenal," says the Clinton national-security adviser, Samuel Berger.

At best, the Clinton system was supposed to block "tens" of rogue-state missiles, while remaining powerless against the 1,000 to 2,000 long-range weapons Russia is expected to maintain. China's 20 single-warhead intercontinental missiles would certainly be at risk. But Clinton officials expected Beijing would build its forces to a size large enough to overwhelm the system—a self-fulfilling prophecy, in critics' eyes.

If Mr. Bush seeks to block only rogue nations, he might continue with the limited Clinton system, with some additions to put his stamp on it. Inertia could be the biggest force favoring this option. The Pentagon already has spent some $7 billion on developing a ground-based system. Planners say that if Mr. Bush gives the order to deploy by this December, they could have the first site's sophisticated radar ready and 20 interceptors on the ground in Alaska as early as 2006.

Most important, the Pentagon has no alternatives even in early stages of development. As part of the effort to woo Russia, the Clinton administration ruled out sea- and space-based national-defense systems, which the ABM treaty clearly bars.

The Clinton system has considerable problems. During the campaign, Mr. Bush criticized its architecture as "inadequate," in part because it can't protect U.S. allies. Other critics say that it would take too long to build and that the remote Alaska site, chosen because it is in the flight path from North Korea, is vulnerable to terrorists or extreme weather. There also are serious questions about whether the technology would work. It has failed two of its first three tests. And 50 Nobel laureates have said it wouldn't be able to distinguish warheads from simple decoys such as balloons.

To address some of the problems, Mr. Bush might add some sea-based missile defenses. In an article in *Washington Quarterly* before he joined the new administration, Deputy National Security Adviser Stephen Hadley called for a "crash program" to transform a few Navy Aegis cruisers currently used to defend ships from short-range missiles. With faster interceptors and new warheads, he said, the ships could be deployed off North Korea's coast to knock out missiles early in their flight.

The Pentagon has done no research on sea-based national defenses. But if they worked, they might solve several problems. A system that hit missiles right after launch would solve the decoy problem, because decoys aren't released until further into flight. It also would pose no real threat to Russia or China, because they could move their missiles inland and out of range. A Mediterranean-based system that hit missiles in mid-course might protect Europe but could remain vulnerable to decoys.

Adding sea-based defenses wouldn't be cheap. A Navy study developed for the new Bush team says the U.S. could build a 12-ship mid-course system to complement ground-based defenses for about $15 billion. Using solely a sea-based system could cost at least three times that much, says an official involved. And neither estimate includes the costs of research and development or of operating the ships.

Mr. Bush has tried to sweeten things for Russia, suggesting deep cuts in U.S. offensive nuclear weapons, an appealing idea to cash-strapped Moscow. But Mr. Hadley's article last year also suggested building four ground-based interceptor sites in all, including one each in Asia and Europe.

Would Moscow go along? The Carnegie Endowment's Joseph Cirincione says that, like the Americans, the Russians are debating whether they want a deal. "One side is arguing that they should use the negotiations to reduce offensive forces and establish rules of the road for missile defenses. The other says 'Let [the Americans] do anything they want. . . . Missile defenses are a fool's game and a waste of money, and let them incur the wrath of the international community.'" As for China, the best way to handle it would likely be an informal but clear understanding that any U.S. system will be limited and that Washington won't overreact if Beijing builds up its arsenal in response.

The world will look very different if Mr. Bush decides he needs a system that can guard against a lot more than just rogue states. And the pressure to go that route may be hard to resist. After years

---

"For how long are we going to allow Russian fears to define our security?"—Former Reagan official Richard Perle

---

of chafing at the ABM treaty, some of his supporters are in no mood to settle for less. "I'm not saying that we should go out of our way to build a defense that's effective against Russia," says Richard Perle, a former Reagan official who advised Mr. Bush during the campaign. "But for how long are we going to allow Russian fears to define our security?"

Russia's military fortunes have so declined that the only Russian threat mentioned seriously in debate is an accidental launch. That could be one of the hardest to defend against, especially if Moscow holds on to its multiple-warhead missiles—a move it has threatened if the U.S. pulls out of the ABM treaty.

Some missile-defense advocates instead see China as the real threat. Their biggest fear isn't of a direct attack but of nuclear blackmail, in which China might try to deter the U.S. from coming to the defense of Taiwan by threatening to attack American cities.

There is no way to build a system based on the size of a future Chinese arsenal, because that size will depend in part on the shape of American defenses. So if Mr. Bush chooses to build a large system, his only limits would be cost and the technology's capability. A newly fashionable phrase among missile-defense supporters is "layered defenses": systems on land, sea, in the air and eventually in outer space, to allow repeated shots at any incoming missile. "My goal would be to do what you can soon . . . and then keep building as the technology becomes available," says Sen. Kyl.

If Mr. Bush decides to layer defenses, he could mix and match—such as by pressing ahead with the land-based system but adding sites and improving accuracy with space-based sensors. If Congress were willing to pay the bill, he could make a parallel push for sea-based defenses. The Air Force is also working to develop an airborne laser that might be able to shoot down missiles early in flight.

For many missile-defense advocates, the jewel in the crown is still Mr. Reagan's vision of a space-based system, though it's anathema to Moscow. The Pentagon has a demonstration program that could put an experimental laser in space by 2012. But fielding such a system could take decades, and no one has a good estimate of cost. In the near term, Mr. Bush would probably increase funding for research into space-based lasers or on small orbiting interceptors, known as Brilliant Pebbles, championed by his father.

Any attempt to put even defensive weapons in space would be highly controversial. Such a system also would be vulnerable to attack. The senior Mr. Bush hoped to overcome both of those flaws with his proposal to share the technology with U.S. allies and the Russians.

Predictions vary on how the world would react if Mr. Bush chose to build a large, treaty-busting system. Missile-defense backers say that with time, U.S. allies and rivals would adjust. But a CIA report prepared for the White House last year outlines some disturbing scenarios, including a possible Chinese nuclear buildup that would spur an arms race in Asia involving India and Pakistan. And it warns that the Russians or Chinese could sell "countermeasures" and other system-busting technology to the likes of North Korea, Iran or Iraq.

A New View of Where America Fits in the World[5]

By David E. Sanger
New York Times, February 18, 2001

Presidential campaigns are a notoriously bad environment for debating how America will approach the world. During the cold war, every candidate sought to prove he would be tough on the Communists, and his opponent a wimp. In this murkier age of global markets, globe-trotting terrorists, disintegrating superpowers and distended peacekeeping missions, George W. Bush made realists happy by assuring them he would protect America's "national interests," while assuring allies that America would stop lecturing and conduct a "more humble foreign policy."

No one was quite certain what it all meant.

But in the past few weeks, Mr. Bush has begun defining his terms, setting his priorities—and in the case of Iraq, giving notice that he may be new to this, but he doesn't plan to show it.

Last week, Mr. Bush set a broad new direction for America's military, told reservists that he would bring a halt to the "overdeployments" of troops around the world, and talked about gas exploration and new immigration policy with President Vincente Fox in Mexico. Most dramatically, he approved an air raid on radar control facilities near Baghdad that he hopes will chasten Saddam Hussein on the eve of Gen. Colin L. Powell's first visit to the Middle East as secretary of state. The raid underscored Mr. Bush's first foreign policy objective: to take command of events overseas, while being far more selective than the Clinton administration about which thickets to enter. That is more an inclination than a strategy, and there are plenty of rough edges.

So far, for example, Mr. Bush's approach to Russia has been somewhat less than humble. In the past few days Defense Secretary Donald Rumsfeld has declared that Moscow's role as an "active proliferator" of missile technology helped propel the White House toward developing a national missile defense—a plan the Russians and Chinese detest. Then there is Treasury Secretary Paul H. O'Neill, who has bluntly declared that the Clinton administration's loans to Russia were "crazy" and has told the Kremlin to pay off the old Soviet Union's debts and forget about new aid until it cleans up rampant corruption.

Mr. O'Neill also says countries like Russia that mismanage their currencies and economies are on their own, and should expect no cash from Washington. On the other hand, he says, Japan will no longer get Clinton-like lectures about how to reverse its decade-long economic decline.

> *"I worry about our ugly-American problem."—*
> **George W. Bush**

This may not add up to a global vision. But it sure sends a message: don't expect us to leave home as often, and don't expect us to whip out our American Express card when we do. It's not isolationist—but it's far less activist than the let's-have-a-summit approach of Bill Clinton. (Iraq, of course, is a special case.)

One of Mr. Bush's senior foreign policy aides put it this way: "The point Bush makes to us in meeting after meeting is that while the U.S. is indeed very powerful and influential, if we are using that power everywhere, we will either cause a backlash or not prove very effective." It is a sentiment Mr. Bush himself expressed last month, just before the inauguration, while touring his ranch in Crawford, Tex., with two reporters. "I worry about our ugly-American problem," he said.

But can he trust that Japan will change the way it runs its economy, or persuade the Arabs and Israelis to talk rather than shoot, without keeping the United States in the prescription-writing business?

"You would be misreading the new administration to think that there is an aggregate decision to ratchet down," said Philip D. Zelikow, the director of the Miller Center of Public Affairs at the University of Virginia and a longtime friend and associate of Condoleezza Rice, Mr. Bush's national security adviser. "The two words they use the most often are discipline and strategy. It comes out of a sense that the Clinton people were too undisciplined, and they let events drive them."

Mr. Bush's team, he argued, is "trying hard to recover choice." That is why this president has no intention of playing the middle in the Israeli-Palestinian conflict, and why he abhors tying up the military in "nation-building," which in his view hurts readiness for emergencies.

All this fits nicely into Mr. Bush's preference for pragmatism over ideology. Like his father, he tends to attack problems through personal relationships—which is what the ranch diplomacy with Mr.

Fox was all about. Perhaps this was Mr. Bush's idea of humility: he talked about a "North American energy policy" rather than one the United States presumes to dominate, and he appeared to be taking seriously proposals for a guest worker program that sends shivers up the backs of some conservatives in his own party.

The flip side of the Bush team's predilection for the personal is a lack of much real enthusiasm for the multilateral institutions that Mr. Clinton saw as the vital wiring of a globalized world.

In his last speech to the United Nations, Mr. Clinton talked about promoting a global rapid-reaction force that, with American help, could intervene inside national borders before civil war turned to genocide. Don't hold your breath for Mr. Bush to repeat those words. As a close military adviser to Vice President Cheney notes, "There's a real sense in this White House that the Haitis and Rwandas and Kosovos of the world are not materially better off after our interventions than they would have been without them."

If that's the analysis, though, Mr. Bush's few weeks in the Oval Office have already taught him to speak with a lot more subtlety than he did on the campaign trail.

For example, there he was last week at NATO's Atlantic headquarters in Norfolk, Va., repeating that he would consult, consult and consult some more before doing anything precipitous about pulling troops out of the Balkans. Similarly, in an exchange of letters with President Jiang Zemin of China last week, he said Beijing had nothing to fear from an American missile defense. He says he is certain he will convince the Chinese, over time, that his plan is not aimed at them.

The fear in Europe and Asia, of course, is that the talk of consultation is just for show—that Mr. Bush wants to put a multinational patina on views he's already arrived at.

"That's not the case," a senior adviser argues. "I am certain that the consultations will affect our plans in a variety of areas."

Of course, the real test of America's new management won't come until grand pronouncements confront some global reality. Iraq is just a start. The first time a Rwanda-like carnage unfolds on CNN, or a Russia-like financial crisis threatens to take out the Nasdaq, the conversations about "overdeployment" and "crazy" financial interventions will get truly interesting. That's also when the president who has been overseas three times in his adult life gets his first real tour of the world.

IV. China and "Rogue States"

This outdoor billboard in Beijing, China, celebrates Chinese laborers.

Editor's Introduction

In an address to Congress, President George W. Bush described 21st-century threats from "rogue states," developing nations that the United States considers a threat to its security and to international stability. To gain "rogue" status, a nation must do most of the following: support terrorism abroad, violate human rights at home, buy and build weapons of mass destruction, and threaten or express hatred for the United States. The rogue states defined by the U.S. government are Iran, Iraq, Libya, North Korea, and Cuba. Although Cuba has no weapons of mass destruction, it is on the list for providing a safe haven for known terrorists and for supporting revolutionary movements in Latin America and elsewhere. To punish and deter the activities of these so-called outlaws, the U.S. employs military force, covert operations, and economic sanctions. The most widely used of these punishments is economic sanctions, which isolate a nation and deprive it of goods. Unfortunately, sanctions do not always work as intended. For example, economic sanctions against Cuba have only strengthened Fidel Castro's position, as he can now blame the American embargo for Cuba's economic disarray; Saddam Hussein also uses this tactic in Iraq.

China, the most powerful communist nation, is occasionally considered a threat to international security because it sells weapons to rogue nations and violates human rights. Many, however, feel this threat is exaggerated, since China is still a developing nation with a weak economy and its weapons are said to be inferior. Because the U.S. government wants positive relations with China, it rarely refers to that country as a rogue nation. Relations with China have grown tense since the Cold War, however, due to controversies surrounding the U.S. spy-plane incident, leaks of U.S. nuclear technology secrets to China, and Chinese arms exports to rogue states. President George W. Bush further fueled post–Cold War tension between the U.S. and China shortly after his inauguration when he said the United States would do "whatever it took" to defend Taiwan if the island were attacked by China. The articles in this section explore issues concerning U.S. relations with China and the rogue states, including whether or not a second Cold War is possible, the importance of establishing normal trade relations with China, U.S. views of Korea and Vietnam, and the wisdom of continuing economic sanctions against Iraq.

In "Back to the Cold War?" Ben Barber wonders whether the U.S. might find itself engaged in a new sort of Cold War in light of a number of international incidents: the collision of a U.S. spy-plane with a Chinese jet fighter; Bush's controversial missile shield proposal, protested by most European governments; and Bush's withdrawal from an international agreement aimed at slowing the pace of climate change. These events, critics say, show evidence of a "backward-looking Bush team," though most experts agree that the Cold War is not coming back, since no country has the resources to challenge the United States military.

Richard Lowry's article, "China Trade—Without Guilt," argues for the importance of trade with China, given that the U.S. itself faces sanctions from the World Trade Organization if it refuses to establish "normal trade relations" with that country. One factor in China's becoming a member of the W.T.O. is that its communist government will have to enact reforms to promote economic growth. Lowry says that a communist China married to a free market could result in the development of capitalist institutions, such as private enterprise and a middle class, and greater respect for international law. In "More Americans Are Ready to Reduce Trade with China," John Dillin reports on the results of a survey (taken shortly after the U.S. spy-plane incident) that suggests most Americans disagree with their government and the W.T.O. when it comes to trading with the Chinese. In addition to the many individuals who admit to boycotting Chinese-made products, others accuse China of limiting U.S. access to its markets, violating human rights, and stealing U.S. intellectual property.

In "Without 'Rogue States' U.S. Strategy Loses Its Focus," Andrew Bacevich explores the political necessity of keeping nations on a "rogue states" list. Bacevich explains that the identification of countries as rogue states, and therefore U.S. adversaries, is a justification for spending on defense and a "rationale for an American military establishment . . . [to prepare] to fight two major wars at the same time." North Korea, seen as the "ultimate rogue," seems poised to establish trade relations with the United States, as the U.S. announces plans to eliminate sanctions against that country. But without the focus on rogue states as enemies, Bacevich claims, the U.S. may lose the incentive for military development and continued preparedness, and open opportunities for new and stronger opponents.

Vietnam's position as a strategic post from which to monitor Chinese activities is the topic of George Wilson's "New Pact Could Foster Military Ties." Wilson compares present-day Vietnam to Turkey, from which the U.S. monitored the Soviet Union during the Cold War. If relations with Vietnam strengthen, the U.S. could gain the same advantage over China as it once had over the Soviet Union.

The last article in this section is an interview by Matthew Rothschild of Denis Halliday, a United Nations specialist in Third World development issues who was appointed U.N. Humanitarian Coordinator in Iraq. Halliday discusses his disapproval of both the economic sanctions imposed against Iraq and the military operations conducted by American and British troops, claiming those actions represent "the brutalization of an innocent people." Halliday advocates lifting the economic sanctions in order to alleviate the suffering of the Iraqi people.

Back to the Cold War?[1]

BY BEN BARBER
SALON.COM, APRIL 3, 2001

The diplomatic furor over the American spy plane forced to land on China's Hainan Island Sunday after bumping into a Chinese warplane appears to confirm that the U.S. is drifting into a time warp that's recreating the grim old days of the Cold War.

Just last month, 50 Russian diplomats were expelled from Washington for spying. Fifty U.S. diplomats got the boot in return by Moscow's president Vladimir Putin, a former KGB spy master. Days earlier, Bush administration officials called North Korea's bizarre Stalinist leader Kim Jong-il nasty names and threatened to break a 1994 nuclear pact with that country.

Nor has George W. Bush spared his allies, pushing them to swallow the National Missile Defense system which Europe detests as unnecessary, expensive and destabilizing. And less than a week ago, Europe was shocked by Bush's withdrawing the U.S. from negotiations over the Kyoto protocol on climate change—a move that had little to do with defense policy, of course, but one that foreign leaders have widely perceived as a throwback to a unilateral, Cold War superpower approach to global problems.

So far no one is sure what's going on. Are the conservative advisors to the inexperienced president trapped in the rhetoric of the past? Are they seeking to advance what they see as America's national interests by taking tough stands that seemed to work during the Reagan years, the Cuban missile crisis or perhaps old westerns like *High Noon*?

Or is this simply a new team finding its way over some bumps in the road—such as the legacy of genuine Russian spies, an intense Chinese fear of U.S. hegemony and North Korea's habit of nuclear blackmail?

Critics blame a backward-looking Bush team. "The Bush administration comes to power with visions of a world akin to that when the Cold War was still going," says former senior Clinton White House policy official Ivo Daalder, now at the Brookings Institution. "They see a world divided into black and white, good and evil. The bad countries are led by despotic, evil or confused people. Russia is led

---

1. This article first appeared in *Salon.com*. Reprinted with permission.

by spies, China by communists, North Korea by a despotic dictator. They believe you have to deal with these people firmly. No pussy-footing. Stand up, respectful but firm."

Other analysts agree that the spy plane impasse is more worrisome against the backdrop of Bush rhetoric about China. "The actual interdicting of U.S. aircraft by the Chinese goes on all the time; it has been for decades, but the current heightened tension began after Bush became president," says Rodger Baker, a senior analyst for *Stratfor.com.* "Bush's team has labeled China as a particular area of concern for Asia, and U.S. leaks of what our new foreign policy and military posture will look like have heightened tensions."

Still, there's no evidence in this specific instance that saber-rattling will take precedence over problem-solving as the Bush team tries to get the plane's crew back safely and resolve the incident.

"I certainly don't think we're entering a new Cold War," says a senior State Department official, speaking on condition of anonymity. "You have a moment where the new administration has not fully formed its ability to carry out our own policy and let us put our own stamp on things. To some extent, we've got to deal with things as they happen. Some are difficult, like the plane thing in China or the spy scandal with Russia.

"Don't think it's the entire policy. If people give it a couple of months they will see a more rounded and more positive policy. There is a desire not to reenter Cold War scenarios."

> *[G. W.] Bush promised a "humble" foreign policy which would not humiliate the less powerful nations of the world— that is, all of the rest of them.*

With or without a Cold War mentality, the United States has enemies and rivals, if not for strategic preeminence then for power and influence and wealth in the smaller theaters of the world. France covets its control over former colonies in West Africa; Russia wants to keep NATO from expanding eastward into the Baltics; India bristles at any outside rival within South Asia; Iran and Islamic terrorists oppose any Western presence in the Persian Gulf region.

But those sizable tensions don't explain the seismic shift between the Bush foreign policy of the campaign trail and the statements made by the White House since President Bush took office. During the campaign, Bush promised a "humble" foreign policy which would not humiliate the less powerful nations of the world—that is, all of the rest of them. The talk was comforting—until Defense Secretary Donald Rumsfeld and National Security Advisor Condoleezza Rice seized control of the dais, and pushed Secretary of State Colin

Powell aside. Now, they say, U.S. policy will be based on "national interest," and there's much less talk about humility than during the campaign—in fact, there's none.

The latest moves are also a far cry from what Colin Powell declared last week—that U.S. policy would be based on U.S. "values." But what, exactly, those values are remains to be resolved. There's an ideological split emerging in the Bush administration between centrists and the right wing of the Republican Party. The battle lines have been drawn, but the winner is not yet clear.

Powell, the centrist, socially liberal black Republican from South Bronx who could have had the nomination from either party for vice president after the Gulf War, offers to continue talks with North Korea. A day later, recall, he was forced to back down. Powell goes to the Middle East with an offer to ease sanctions on Iraqi consumer goods if Arab allies, reassured Iraqi suffering is being eased, will tighten arms controls on Baghdad. Back in Washington, Republican hawks call him a chicken for easing any sanctions.

The Cheney-Rumsfeld-Bush team may seek to rekindle some other Cold War battlefields.

Even back when he was a general and chairman of the Joint Chiefs of Staff, Powell was more liberal than Vice President Dick Cheney, who was then defense secretary. In Powell's autobiography, *My American Journey*, he recalls trying to convince Cheney to get rid of tactical nuclear artillery shells.

"Not one of my civilian advisors supports you," Cheney responded.

"I kidded him," Powell writes: "That's because they're all right-wing nuts like you."

The Cheney-Rumsfeld-Bush team may seek to rekindle some other Cold War battlefields. It's not hard to imagine them resurrecting Savimbi's rebels in Angola, tilting away from democratic India to Cold War ally Pakistan, or restoring aid to repressive militaries in Indonesia and Guatemala. And aid to Colombia's drug war could quickly expand to aid in fighting leftist guerrillas. Covert actions could be taken to support center-right and rightist candidates while undermining center-left and leftists in places like Nicaragua, Haiti, Honduras and Central Asia.

Ivo Daalder says there is no doubt a tug-of-war going on between Powell and the right. "Rumsfeld seems to consistently win because Cheney and Rice are in his camp," he suggests. "Powell seems to be the odd man out."

The State Department official denies the existence of any rift. "I don't think there is any evidence that Rumsfeld is on the right of Powell," he says. "Powell is with the president on all these issues. You take a guy like Powell who talks about these things and juxtapose him with guys who are not out there so much and you will have some disagreements—but not in their fundamental approach. The president fundamentally does not want to restart the Cold War."

Les Gelb, president of the Council on Foreign Relations, agrees. "The Cold War is not coming back," Gelb says in a telephone interview from New York. "Even if there is an increase in tension with Russia and China, neither one has the will or the resources to confront the United States around the world. Relations can get nasty, but not dangerous as they did in the Cold War," he says.

Gelb reminds us that the Cold War was a time when the U.S. mainland was threatened with a flaming, radioactive, nuclear holocaust. These days, even if a Russian, a Serb, a Chinese or an Iranian might dream of such an attack, they are all but incapable of mounting one, Gelb asserts. So the new tensions between old Cold War adversaries are tempests in a teapot compared to the real Cold War.

"I don't think Rumsfeld and Cheney are unreconstructed Cold Warriors," says Gelb. "They're smart guys."

Yet Daalder sees a mentality that's similar to what led U.S. hawks—including current Defense Secretary Donald Rumsfeld—to form the Committee on the Present Danger in the 1970s and 1980s, in order to warn of the Soviet threat. Today, of course, Russia is but a shadow of its former self—its economy in ruins, its people dying faster than they are born and its military rusting away. It's got nuclear weapons but no bread and medicine. Daalder fears that by hyping the threats from Russia, the Bush administration could create a self-fulfilling prophesy.

"If we treat them as enemies they become enemies, especially because Russia, China and North Korea are in transition" toward free-market and less-repressive societies, he says. "By keeping Russia at arm's length we do not encourage them to cooperate on foreign policy. By calling China a competitor we do not encourage cooperation. By not engaging North Korea we do not encourage more reasonable behavior."

And while the Bush team tries to install its players and write new policies even as things fall apart around it, and petty tyrants from Iraq or North Korea see how far they can get with the new administration, there is a growing chorus of critics who warn that the China threat is an incipient new Cold War.

Not only is China the rising power in Asia, it is the one country that openly dismisses the United States as a role model, seeking to modernize economically but keep tight social and political control over its 1.3 billion people. It also defies U.S. efforts to stop weapons proliferation, selling nuclear, missile and other technologies to North Korea, Pakistan and Iran.

According to a recent publication by Michael Pillsbury, a China analyst at National Defense University, there's a power struggle going on inside China that is far greater than the one some believe separates Powell and Rumsfeld. Pillsbury's book, *China Debates the Future Security Environment*, reports that Chinese hawks believe the United States is morally bankrupt and ready to fall within a decade or two.

And while Chinese soft-liners on the U.S. urge their nation to lie low and try to lull the Americans into submission, lest American hard-liners try to transform China into our new enemy, Chinese hard-liners compare Americans to Nazis and wild beasts, and urge a much tougher stance.

This gulf in thinking perplexes U.S. military analysts, who are unsure just who is in charge in Beijing. They try to read actions such as the close pursuit of U.S. electronic spy planes as a sign of hard-liner tactics.

U.S. military officials say that in recent weeks they had warned the Chinese not to fly so aggressively when following the U.S. patrols, which they say take place over international water. This is in itself an issue, since China claims as its own a vast swath of the South China Sea—which is also claimed by Vietnam, the Philippines and other countries. The United States considers it international waters. It was over these contested waters that the planes collided, sending the Chinese plane and pilot into the sea where the pilot remains missing.

Meanwhile, Bush said yesterday he is not pleased that there has been no U.S. contact with the crew of 24 men and women, and neither has he been assured the Chinese will respect the integrity of the aircraft and not enter it.

U.S. offers to help in search and rescue efforts for the Chinese pilots went unanswered. Bush himself failed to answer a question yesterday shouted at him by a reporter on the White House lawn: "Are the crew hostages?"

China Trade—Without Guilt[2]

It Is Logical, Moral, and Right.

BY RICHARD LOWRY
NATIONAL REVIEW, MAY 14, 2001

It's quite an accomplishment to do the bidding of U.S. corporations and accept Marxist premises at the very same time. But this is the nifty trick pulled off by advocates of free trade with China, at least according to their critics. Congress will vote again this summer on granting "normal trade relations" to China. Passage of NTR seems all but certain. But, especially in light of China's recent eleven-day experiment in taking U.S. servicemen hostage, the trade vote will be the object of kitchen-sink criticism from left and right, alleging that corporations bought the vote with soft-money donations, that it is an expression of a crude economic determinism, even that it represents an act of "appeasement" worthy of Neville Chamberlain at his Hitler-coddling worst.

China trade risks becoming the least reputable measure to win wide congressional support since the bankruptcy bill (which passed the Senate in March by a 85–15 vote, but is still portrayed as a practically medieval effort to bleed the poor). This is a shame. Trade with China has self-interested, and not particularly subtle or savory, backers in the business community. But this says nothing about the merits of the free-trade measures in question. Economic engagement with China serves to foster pockets of liberty in China, and possibly to undermine its regime at its roots. What critics—a collection of union protectionists and human-rights advocates on the left and economic nationalists and neoconservative defense hawks on the right—offer in its stead is a policy of economic isolation that has failed elsewhere, and would be applied to China mostly as a matter of moral dudgeon: irritable gesture masquerading as strategy.

The China-trade debate features a parade of initials. For more than a decade, China was granted "most favored nation" (MFN) status after an annual debate on Capitol Hill. Last year, the MFN debate became the NTR debate, in a change of nomenclature to reflect the fact that "favored" trade status is enjoyed by almost all nations in the world and therefore is more appropriately called "normal." Meanwhile, China has moved closer to joining the World Trade Organization (WTO). Members of the WTO aren't permitted to conduct annual reviews of each other's trade status, so when China joins this free-trade group, it must be granted permanent NTR (PNTR) by the United States (unless the U.S. wants to risk WTO sanctions). As part of its WTO entry, China in 1999 agreed to cut tariffs and restrictions on American agriculture, industrial products, banking, insurance, telecommunications, and movies, and to make other economic reforms.

This is good news, and not just because Coca-Cola executives have

---

Gauging the influence of the state on the Chinese economy is difficult because China's market is about as transparent as the Great Wall.

---

visions of 1 billion potential smiles. The question of how to change China is essentially the question of how to starve and make irrelevant the biggest welfare state in the world. As its ideology has collapsed into a shell of its former self, the Communist government has turned to economic growth as the way to preserve its legitimacy. But this is a gamble, as sustaining growth means allowing private initiative, establishing the rule of law, and tolerating the creation of a middle class. So, the Chinese regime is increasingly committed to the notion that it can be a little bit pregnant, that a Communist dictatorship can, more or less, depend on the workings of the free market for its support.

It's a risk. One example: As former Heritage Foundation analyst Stephen J. Yates, now in Vice President Cheney's office, has written, "State workers are forced to depend on government-subsidized benefits. Because they are not paid enough to be able to choose private alternatives, they must comply with intrusive government regulations, like family planning and controls on speech, or risk the loss of vital benefits." This means anything that creates employment opportunities outside the state sector potentially reduces this pressure point for the regime. And this has been the trajectory of development since [the] late 1970s, when the state accounted for almost all economic output. Estimates differ on the exact figure now, but state-owned businesses are only part of the picture.

China, of course, shouldn't be mistaken for Hong Kong. Gauging the influence of the state on the Chinese economy is difficult because China's market is about as transparent as the Great Wall.

The government tries to get its tentacles into any sizable economic enterprise, and many shrewd entrepreneurs include bureaucrats in their businesses from the start for protection. Managers of a given business may not even know who owns their firm, so shadowy is this stew of crony communism and capitalism. On top of all this confusion, the regime desperately works to keep its inefficient and failing state-run businesses afloat, with loans from state banks that act as perpetual subsidies—think of the U.S. Postal Service with "Chinese characteristics."

Economic engagement with China will tend to tip this mess in a positive direction. The WTO, for instance, will open the Chinese market to Western banks. Today Chinese banks can afford their incontinent lending practices because they have a captive savings market. Chinese workers must accept the rotten deal they get from these socialist dinosaurs. But when, say, Chase Manhattan shows up, this may no longer be the case, and Chinese banks, a linchpin of the state sector, will be subject to competitive pressures. In general, trade will create, from both foreign and Chinese businessmen, pressure to establish transparent rules for economic transactions—to create beach-heads, in short, for the rule of law.

Economic liberty, the rule of law, and privately held wealth are all crucial ingredients to political liberalization. But suggesting a relationship between economic development and liberalization is often dismissed by critics as a quasi-Marxist economic determinism. Instead, it is watered-down John Locke: The connection between economic liberty and political liberty is central to the most admirable strain of Western political thought. The correlation between the two is also a fact. The neoconservative Project for the New American Century in a 1999 memo opposing MFN called the connection "an interesting theory, but just a theory." It would be more accurate to say it's an observation, based on, among other things, the recent history of Asia.

The Growth Effect

It is Taiwan—on whose behalf critics of China trade sometimes say the mainland needs to be isolated—that is the prime exhibit for the political benefits of economic growth. As Taiwan became steadily more economically advanced and integrated into the world economy over the last thirty years, it also progressed from a one-party system to the constitutional democracy of today. South Korea followed roughly the same path. As the Hoover Institution's Henry S. Rowen has noted, countries tend to tip into democracies when their per capita annual GDP reaches $5,000 to $7,000. "Spain, Portugal, Chile, and Argentina, in addition to Taiwan and South Korea," Rowen writes, "all made the transition to democracy while they were in this income range."

If current trends hold, China will reach this level of wealth in fifteen to twenty years. This doesn't mean that China will join the WTO, then immediately break out the Magna Carta. The regime will bully, cheat, kill, and maim, in an effort to resist political liberalization every step of the way. (Its model may be Singapore, a rich one-party state—although one, it's worth noting, that allows considerable personal and economic liberty.) Indeed, as economic growth increases the possibility of personal freedom, it will also create more occasions for repression in China. Trade will not directly change the regime, but instead the society around it, thus creating the conditions for liberalization over the long haul.

> **China is not the Soviet Union, let alone Nazi Germany.**

Critics of China trade don't have the patience to wait for this long-term loosening and instead want the gratification of doing something, of isolating China, now. In a sense, the post-World War II period has already been a test of these two rival approaches. As Owen Harries has written in *The National Interest*, "For more than two decades—from 1949 to the early 1970s—the United States tried containing and, within its means, isolating China. That period was one of the most disastrous not only in Chinese history but in all of human history: a ruthless tyranny prevailed, millions of Chinese were killed by the regime or died because of its insane policies, obscurantism ruled, the economy was reduced to a shambles. Internationally, China actively supported subversion and insurrection throughout its region, fought a war against India, and even tried its hand at intervention in Africa."

But China's progress from a regime of mass murder thirty years ago to one of nasty repression barely registers for the more vehement critics of NTR. Indeed, the same way that it is perpetually Selma for Jesse Jackson, it is always Munich for some neoconservatives. Is the question whether to confront in Kosovo an ineffectual Balkan dictator who has already lost two or three wars? Munich! Whether to establish permanent trade relations with China? Munich, again! This is more a verbal tic than an argument. China is not the Soviet Union, let alone Nazi Germany. China doesn't have an alternative ideology with global appeal. It isn't fighting the United States on every possible front worldwide, and couldn't do so even if it wanted to. It is essentially a Third World country, with a per capita income that badly trails Taiwan's.

Of course, China's trade with the world will change this, and provide the regime more funds for the purchase of new weapons systems. What critics of China trade fail to acknowledge is that it is not in the power of the United States to stop this long-term trend. The American export market is extremely important, but China—like 19th-century America—is benefiting from a burgeoning domestic market as well. America can't wave a wand and stop Chinese growth in its tracks. China is going to join the WTO no matter what. And Europe, Japan, and other Asian countries wouldn't go along with an American effort to cut off trade with China. For instance, roughly 40,000 Taiwanese companies have $40 billion invested in China. What critics of China trade are proposing is, essentially, that America become more Taiwanese than Taiwan.

> *What critics of China trade are proposing is . . . that America become more Taiwanese than Taiwan.*

Even if it were in Washington's power to block all trade with China, it wouldn't be wise policy. The Americas offer two—imperfect of course—case studies in the effects of trade policy. Tiny Cuba, just 90 miles away, has been isolated by the United States for four decades, but Castro remains stubbornly in place. Meanwhile, Mexico has advanced toward a full-blown liberal democracy, with an assist from the liberalizing effects of NAFTA. If economic sanctions were effective, Iraq, North Korea, Vietnam, and Burma, among others, would be teeming pluralistic societies by now. It's not true that sanctions never work—South Africa is arguably a case where they did—but economic growth and liberalization have a much better record of prompting political reform.

During the debate last year over granting PNTR to China, trade critics complained that the United States would lose the "leverage" it gained from the annual review under the old MFN process. It is true that every year around the time of the MFN vote, China would release dissidents from prison, in a clumsy and obvious PR gesture. But this didn't represent any serious loosening of the regime's grip. And this American "leverage" was dependent on trading with China in the first place—otherwise, there would be nothing to threaten to cut off. In any case, the U.S. should realize the limits of its ability to fine-tune internal Chinese politics as if it were adjusting the FM dial. Cutting off normal trade relations with China won't cause the regime to sink to its knees, while trade and economic growth will help create the conditions for liberalization in China, though not guarantee it.

Trade critics like to pretend otherwise. Take a *Weekly Standard* editorial by William Kristol and Robert Kagan at the time of the PNTR vote last year, with an epitaph quoting (of course) Winston

Churchill warning against appeasement. "In the coming weeks and months" after the vote, they warned, more members of the Falun Gong and Tibetan Buddhists would be arrested: "Let those who voted for permanent trade status for China explain then what a boon it was for Chinese freedom." But no one is suggesting that free trade with China will cause freedom to blossom in the next "weeks and months." Nor should trade with China make advocates of PNTR responsible for every act of cruelty on the mainland.

Limiting U.S. trade with China would ultimately—since there is little hope that other nations would go along, let alone that it would sink the regime—be about expressing U.S. frustration and outrage with China. This moral disapproval has its place, but shouldn't come at the cost of a policy that is marginally increasing freedom in China. The U.S. should maintain a drumbeat of criticism of China's repressive practices, and should send its sternest message through a tough-minded security policy in the region. Trade critics worry that American corporations doing business in China will lobby for a softer line on the dictatorship. This is a real worry, but is nothing that can't be overcome by determined advocacy. The same Congress that is supposedly wholly owned by corporate interests when it comes to China voted 341–70 last year to pass the Taiwan Security Enhancement Act that tilted U.S. policy toward the tiny democracy.

A policy of trading with China may not be emotionally satisfying, as it requires waiting for an arrogant and nasty dictatorship to be entangled in, and perhaps brought down by, its own economic ambitions. But—and this may be the highest recommendation for any policy—it is better than the alternative. "To get rich is glorious," Deng Xiaoping famously said. His dictatorial successors may—eventually—discover that it's not quite as glorious as he thought.

More Americans Are Ready To Reduce Trade With China[3]

BY JOHN DILLIN
CHRISTIAN SCIENCE MONITOR, MAY 15, 2001

If the product says "Made in China," many Americans have begun to put it back on the store shelf.

Public dismay with China is growing. More people are boycotting Chinese-made goods since the tense April incident involving an American reconnaissance plane. And many in the United States are beginning to question Washington's long effort, begun in 1979, to expand trade with Beijing.

A nationwide poll reports new, worrisome signs for U.S.-China trade relations. Among the findings:

• A plurality of Americans now says that bilateral trade between the United States and China should be reduced.

• More than 20 percent of Americans say they shun any products made in China. That has increased from 15 percent a month ago.

• Republicans, who normally support expanded relations, are among those most strongly in favor of reducing trade with China.

The Christian Science Monitor/TIPP poll, conducted May 3 to 7, found that 42 percent of Americans want to see China trade at lower levels than it is today. Only 33 percent would keep trade at current levels. The other 25 percent are unsure.

Foes of trade with China were often critical of that country's record on human rights.

A communications technician in Arizona, one of 904 adults interviewed for the Monitor/TIPP study, says he would favor revoking China's favorable trade status "because of its abysmal record on human rights." But he worries that unless other countries joined the effort, it might not be effective.

The April crisis over the U.S. military reconnaissance plane that made an emergency landing on Hainan Island exacerbated relations between the two countries and came at a time when concern was mounting about the huge U.S. trade deficit with China.

Ten years ago, China sold products to the U.S. worth $19 billion while it purchased $6.3 billion in U.S. goods—a U.S. deficit of $12.7 billion.

By 2000, China sold the U.S. $100.1 billion in goods, while it purchased only $16.3 billion—a record deficit for the U.S. with China of $83.8 billion.

American officials have encouraged this expansion of trade in hopes that the U.S. will eventually win its fair share of the consumer market in the world's most populous country. A March report by the Congressional Research Service states: "Many trade analysts

---

From toys to shower curtains, it's often difficult to find a specific product in the U.S. that is not made in China.

---

argue that China could prove to be a significant market for U.S. exports in the future. China is one of the world's fastest growing economies.

"It is projected that by the year 2005, China will have more than 230 million middle-income consumers. If achieved, this would likely make China the world's largest market for consumer goods and services and a major market for luxury goods."

China's trade surplus with the U.S. has provided a cash infusion there that has helped Beijing build its industrial base, lifted the incomes of millions of China's citizens, and furnished additional funding to upgrade its military.

China has also welcomed billions of dollars of investments by corporate giants such as Eastman Kodak, Motorola, BP Amoco, General Motors, and Bank of America.

U.S. companies have been signing contracts at the rate of about $6 billion a year to erect new factories and make other investments in China, though the actual U.S. outlays for plants and equipment in China have run only about two-thirds of that amount.

John Foarde, vice president of the U.S.-China Business Council in Washington, says there is very little evidence so far that the Hainan Island incident has disrupted the two countries' intertwined business ties.

Looking beyond Hainan, Mr. Foarde says the council hopes to build long-term business-to-business relationships with China so robust that "when we have a problem like this, it doesn't swamp everything else."

One factor that works in Beijing's favor is the way Chinese exports have so thoroughly penetrated the U.S. market. From toys to shower curtains, it's often difficult to find a specific product in the U.S. that is not made in China.

China's leading exports to the U.S. last year were toys and games ($19.4 billion), office and data machines ($11 billion), telecommunications and recording equipment ($9.9 billion), footwear ($9.2 billion), and electrical machinery and appliances ($9.1 billion).

The U.S. has actively encouraged this expansion of imports even though China is widely accused by critics of limiting U.S. access to its markets, using prison labor to produce goods for export, violating the rights of religious minorities, and stealing U.S. intellectual property.

Despite public uneasiness about China, there is little expectation here that Congress will revoke China's favored trade status when the issue comes up for a vote in the near future.

Too much trade with China?

Should the U.S. continue to trade with China at current levels, or do you think trade with China should be reduced?

Not sure	25%
Current level	33%
Reduce	42%

The preference for reducing China trade is strongest among people 45 to 64 years old, Republicans, and those who are invested in the stock market. Young adults, Democrats, and noninvestors are the least inclined to want to curb China trade. The poll shows the breakdown, among those who favor reducing trade by:

Age

18–24	25%
25–44	44%
45–64	48%
65 and over	42%

Stock-market participation

Investors	46%
Noninvestors	39%

Political Affiliation

Democrats	40%
Republicans	46%
Independents	41%

Without "Rogue States" U.S. Strategy Loses Its Focus[4]

By Andrew J. Bacevich
Wall Street Journal, June 22, 2000

The visit to North Korea by South Korean president Kim Dae Jung, an excursion that signals a possible reconciliation between these once-implacable foes, is but the latest development to expose the rickety foundations of U.S. national security strategy.

The main premise underlying that strategy—reiterated endlessly by senior officials in the Clinton administration, and endorsed also by influential Republicans—is that the end of the Cold War has given rise to a new security environment. In a post-ideological age, with globalization propelling nations toward a liberal democratic utopia, the bad old notions of power politics no longer apply. Why, given half a chance, entrepreneurs could put soldiers out of business. In the meantime, the chief rationale for maintaining American military strength has been to keep in check those few holdouts that resist the logic of history.

The threat posed by "rogue states" is offered as Exhibit A by those who advance this argument. Yet objectively, the various countries lumped together in this category would seem to pose a negligible challenge to U.S. security—an Iraq weakened by a decade of sanctions and periodic bombing; a Cuba stripped of superpower patronage; and the battered rump of Yugoslavia.

North Korea has always served as the example with which to douse this skepticism. That the Stalinist regime in Pyongyang—ruled by the reclusive and probably nutty Kim Jong Il—was unpredictable, untrustworthy and irredeemable was a position that was hard to argue against. The most militarized country on earth, North Korea stood poised to rain destruction on Seoul. Were that not bad enough, the country exported its weapons to anyone willing to pay the bill, including other bad actors like Iran. And since North Korea was also hellbent on its own nuclear capability, along with missiles of intercontinental range, it came to be seen as the rogue state par excellence.

How this image meshed with that of a country teetering perennially on the brink of mass starvation was never fully explained. But no matter. As long as the notion of North Korea as ultimate rogue remained intact, so too would the need to station 37,000 U.S. troops in the South. And more broadly, so too would the rationale for an American military establishment organized and equipped to fight two major wars simultaneously, one on the Korean peninsula and another against a rogue elsewhere.

Now, in one dramatic gesture, Kim Dae Jung has appeared to explode that rationale. The ultimate rogue now turns out to be a party with whom we can do business. And the "we" includes, most emphatically, the Clinton administration, which has been dealing quietly with Pyongyang for some time, and which has now announced plans to dismantle longstanding U.S. sanctions against the North. Coca-Cola has already shipped its first cases of soft drinks to the North.

The U.S. needs military power not because the "new" environment harbors a finite set of dangers, but because competition for power continues unabated.

The apparent deflation of the threat from North Korea has sent the State Department in search of new phraseology: the term "rogue states," it seems, is to be discarded in favor of the more relaxed-sounding "states of concern." Having articulated a specious original rationale for maintaining American military power, an administration intent on leaving a peacemaker's legacy is now dismantling that rationale.

The Clinton administration eagerly pursues detente with Iran. It signals its willingness to consider honorable retirement for Slobodan Milosevic. It commends Syria for having made a "strategic choice for peace." Concerned about nuclear proliferation? After all the angry words and gestures directed at Pakistan and India in reaction to their nuclear tests, Washington appears to have decided that it would rather coach those countries into becoming responsible members of the nuclear club than demonize them.

In short, we are being told that the ostensible dangers that have defined the "new" security environment are now less scary than previously advertised. But in suggesting that military power is now of declining relevance, the Clinton administration could be courting disaster. In fact, the U.S. needs military power not because the "new" environment harbors a finite set of dangers, but because competition for power continues unabated. That competition determines the shape of the international order. And despite assumptions that history is headed toward some pre-determined destination that coincides neatly with American interests, others harbor views of history that mesh imperfectly, at best, with our own.

Trends in places like the Korean peninsula appear promising not because the old rogues have become trustworthy, but because one particular state—the U.S.—remains dominant in the post–Cold War era. Forfeit the powerful capabilities that underwrite that dominance and you forfeit the equally powerful benefits that derive from it. Utopian illusions that cause Americans to lose sight of the importance of maintaining their military strength can only invite unpleasant surprises. And these will come not from "rogue states," who are of little actual importance, but from the more serious competitors who do not share our illusions.

Vietnam: New Pact Could Foster Military Ties[5]

By George C. Wilson
National Journal, July 22, 2000

The triumph of capitalism over communism in the recently negotiated American-Vietnamese trade agreement brought back memo-
ries of the most embarrassing question I was ever asked during my
two tours as a reporter covering the Vietnam War.

The question came from a South Vietnamese high school teacher
who pulled me off a hot Danang street and invited me into his cool
home. "How come you Americans tell us that this war is capitalism
against communism when your President has his arm around the
biggest communist of them all?" the teacher asked.

It was February 1972. Thousands of South Vietnamese soldiers
allied with the United States were dying at the hands of North Vietnamese communists. Yet President Nixon was in Beijing meeting
with Mao Tse-tung, the Chinese communist dictator who fathered
the economic disaster that was the Great Leap Forward in the '50s
and the bloody Cultural Revolution of the '60s and '70s.

The agitated teacher elaborated on his anguish after offering me
tea. "I tell my students that this war is capitalism vs. communism
and that they should join the army and die for the cause if necessary. How can I tell them that now? Is this war only being fought so
your factories can sell ammunition?"

I could come up with no satisfying answer. I was beginning to see
clearer through the teacher's end of the telescope than through my
own. The exchange, like so many others on the ground in Vietnam,
left both parties troubled and wondering.

Three years after that conversation in Danang, the communists
won the Vietnam War on the battlefield. How ironic it must be to
that South Vietnamese teacher, who saw so many of his students
die in what he considered the capitalist cause, that the communist
leaders won the war but lost the peace. They recently signed a very
capitalistic trade agreement because they realized their nation
would otherwise die economically. "They really had no choice," said
one Vietnamese scholar.

How ironic, too, for the late Nguyen Co Thach, the Vietnamese for-eign minister who told me during a visit to Hanoi in 1990 that "it is stupid" for his country not to adopt the market practices of the West, especially for farmers who needed the motivation of capitalist profits to grow bumper crops of rice. Communist rulers eventually found Thach too radical and tossed him aside.

The agreement on trade will no doubt be followed by other new Washington-Hanoi ties, including a slow but probably sure widen-ing of the military-to-military relationships between the United States and Vietnam. The thin edge of this entering wedge is likely to be quiet exchanges between American and Vietnamese military leaders. This is not unusual, nor unwelcome. The U.S. military qui-etly hosted Russian officers at American military bases bristling with weapons during the Cold War. Letting them see what we could do for—or to—them was part of deterrence.

Diplomats in the United States and Vietnam can build on these increased economic bonds as well as on the natural camaraderie of soldiers who have fought together in the mud. I saw firsthand an example of this camaraderie in 1990 when American and Vietnam-ese writers, who had once been soldiers shooting at each other 25 years earlier, gathered in Hanoi to read their writings to one another. Nervous communist officials tried to keep the exchanges formal and distant. They succeeded until the old foes found the shelves of Heineken beer tucked away in the Politiburo's meeting hall. The pop-pop of cans opening was soon followed by brothers-in-arms laughter and by solemn proclamations, delivered with Ameri-can and Vietnamese arms thrown around each other, such as this one: "Next time let the governments fight. You and I will stay home."

If trade and military relationships flourish on parallel tracks—something American leaders should promote—Vietnam in the long term could become the Turkey of the Far East for the United States. Throughout the Cold War, Turkey was a crucial listening and watching post. Immensely important information coming from mountaintop radar in Turkey told us about Soviet missile tests, for example. U.S. intelligence chiefs would love to have radar on Viet-nam's mountains peering into China. And how much would the United States pay Vietnam to let American warships use its magnif-icent, strategically located port at Cam Ranh Bay? A lot.

Just as today's communist leaders in Hanoi realized that they had to embrace the capitalistic practices in the trade agreement or die on the vine, tomorrow's—if not today's—Vietnamese leaders can be made to see the advantages of broadening military relationships with the United States. Helping them reach that conclusion will be the sight of their ancient enemy, China, galloping into the future with advanced weapons that only the United States can counter.

Beyond the hoopla about the economic world changing for the United States and Vietnam with the signing of the trade agreement are these significant yet so far unmentioned possibilities. It is virtually certain that this pact will also change the military world for the two countries, sooner or later.

Interview: Denis Halliday[6]

BY MATTHEW ROTHSCHILD
THE PROGRESSIVE, FEBRUARY 1, 1999

You probably have heard of Scott Ritter, the UNSCOM weapons inspector (and former U.S. Marine) who resigned his post last August to protest what he saw as the failure of the United States to act more forcefully against Saddam Hussein's weapons of mass destruction. But you may not have heard of Denis Halliday, who resigned his post as head of the United Nations' Oil for Food program in Iraq just weeks later to protest the humanitarian costs of the U.N. sanctions.

"Four thousand to 5,000 children are dying unnecessarily every month due to the impact of sanctions," he said. "We are in the process of destroying an entire society. It is as simple and terrifying as that. It is illegal and immoral."

Halliday, an Irishman, worked for the United Nations for thirty-four years. A specialist in Third World development issues, he was stationed in Iran, Malaysia, and Indonesia, as well as at U.N. headquarters in New York. On September 1, 1997, he was appointed U.N. Humanitarian Coordinator in Iraq. He resigned thirteen months later.

I interviewed him on my radio program, *Second Opinion*, when he came through Madison, Wisconsin, on December 5. And I spoke with him again on the phone later in the month after the United States and Britain bombed Iraq.

Q: Why did you decide to resign from the United Nations?

Denis Halliday: I found myself in the very uncomfortable position of representing the United Nations, which in Iraq has two faces. One is the face of the military inspections supported by sanctions, which are killing thousands of Iraqis every month and sustaining malnutrition at the rate of 30 percent for children alone. At the same time, I'm trying to run a humanitarian assistance program, and I find these two functions incompatible. I don't believe the Security Council has the right to punish the people of Iraq simply because it is unhappy with the president of the country.

Q: You have said that the sanctions policy is a breach of international law. How?

---

6. Article by Matthew Rothschild from *The Progressive* February 1, 1999. Copyright © *The Progressive*. Reprinted with permission.

Halliday: It's a complete breach of the Convention of the Rights of the Child, for example. It's a breach of the Universal Declaration of Human Rights. It undermines the very charter of the United Nations itself. The preamble of the charter is being clobbered by these U.N. sanctions: the right of individuals to have a life, liberty, opportunities to live, work, and so on. It's very fundamental stuff.

Q: What is the magnitude of the suffering in Iraq? I've seen a lot of numbers. I saw one U.N. study that said 500,000 Iraqi children had died—this was several years back—as the result of sanctions.

Halliday: I believe the 500,000 is a UNICEF figure. It's probably closer now to 600,000 and that's over the period of 1990–1998. If you include adults, it's well over one million Iraqi people.

Q: What caused these deaths? What is the chain of fatality?

Halliday: It originates with the horrendous and comprehensive damage done by the missiles and bombing of the coalition forces during the Gulf War period, which was of greater extent than any of us understand. They set about demolishing the civilian infrastructure of this country, including the water supplies, sewage supply systems, electric power systems, the production systems, educational facilities, places of work. It's hard to visualize, perhaps, but the infrastructure that supports a good standard of living has been demolished. So that's the starting point. And then you have the sanctions now for seven or eight years, and the damage that was done, combined with the lack of money, or spare parts, upkeep for maintenance in the agricultural sector. This combined has got us in the situation now where we have poor nutritional intake, we have very poor health services, lack of drugs and medicines, and we have a disastrous water/sewage situation whereby water-borne diseases like typhus are killing thousands of Iraqis, particularly children.

Q: Were you an eyewitness to this hardship?

Halliday: Yes, almost every evening driving back from the office I would have to drive through raw sewage, which was often on the streets of Baghdad. I would come up against three- or four-year-old children begging for money at the traffic lights. And, of course, I visited the poor parts of the country outside Baghdad, and I visited the children's hospital.

Q: What was the hospital like?

Halliday: The conditions are quite appalling. When I was there, there was raw sewage in the basement of this hospital. The doctors do not have drugs to deal with the problems they face. I was looking at young children with leukemia. And of the four children that I got to know in the fall of 1997, two died within six weeks. That's a very common situation: Doctors are making horrible decisions as to who dies, who lives.

Q: What reaction do you get when you go around and speak about the calamity of sanctions?

Halliday: When regular, ordinary people like you and me, so to speak, understand some of the impact, and when they realize that Iraqi people are just like you and me, with all the expectations we have for our children, it hits home that we are rather callously

> *[The Iraqis] have the same expectations we have—to live a life.*

sitting back here and allowing people like ourselves to be killed. But having demonized Saddam Hussein, policy-makers in Washington have demonized the Iraqi people. And they are just regular people, like you and me, with families, and gardens, and dogs, and houses, and all of that stuff. They have the same expectations we have—to live a life.

Q: What was your reaction to the U.S. and British bombing campaign against Iraq in December?

Halliday: I must say, I'm appalled that here we are in 1998 and we are resorting to the brutalization of an innocent people. I find this incredible. Apart from that, I really am concerned that nobody thinks through the consequences of these sorts of actions. There is a bankruptcy here of ideas on how to deal with this country, and bombing is the fall-back position, unfortunately.

It was a totally counterproductive effort. It enhanced Saddam Hussein's image. It outraged the Arab community. It reinforced the general sense that Washington doesn't understand the Arab world. Arabs who heard all the talk from the Clinton Administration about respecting Ramadan—they thought that was a joke. It's done incredible damage to Tony Blair and discredited him in the eyes of the international community. It astonishes me that the U.K. is willing to be led around by the nose, and I find that incompatible with the past role of Great Britain. Britain has distinguished Arabists who understand how the Arab world functions, and I thought they would have come up with something more positive.

Q: What do you make of Richard Butler, head of UNSCOM?

Halliday: I think Butler's finished. He bugs everyone. He's making decisions without consulting Security Council members. He's so much in the pocket of Washington. They own him. They appointed him. He's their man. He's Madeleine Albright's creation.

Q: Let's take the argument of Scott Ritter, Richard Butler, and Madeleine Albright. They say, "Look, Saddam Hussein used weapons of mass destruction against Kurds and Iranians, and he invaded Kuwait. If it weren't for economic sanctions, as punitive as they've been, Saddam Hussein would have more of these weapons of mass destruction right now."

Halliday: Well, you know, you have to perhaps start at the beginning and query, "Where did these arms come from in the first

---

Nothing justifies . . . the decision by the Security Council to kill and maim Iraqi people to the tune of thousands every month.

---

place?" I think Saddam Hussein was an ally of the West, and this country in particular, when he took on the battle with Iran. He was a good guy, and now of course, he's not a good guy. And I am not about to apologize for him or support him. However, nothing justifies, in my view, the decision by the Security Council to kill and maim Iraqi people to the tune of thousands every month.

Q: You seem much less worried than a lot of U.S. officials about the danger of someone like Saddam Hussein acquiring these weapons of mass destruction. Why does that seem not to trouble you so much? Or, if you're troubled, why do you think that a different approach is necessary?

Halliday: You know, I think no matter how we make this work, there's going to be a risk factor. But I believe that if we are going to move forward, we have to separate economic sanctions—which only hurt the people, not the leadership—from the issue of the rearming of Iraq. Separate those two things and deal with them separately.

Q: And how do you ensure that Iraq doesn't cheat?

Halliday: You need an elaborate system of control on the manufacture and purchases of military items. The Iraqis will have to understand that there would be a need to monitor military rebuilding well after sanctions have gone. I think that would have to be one of the arrangements.

Q: By your own estimation, what is the extent of Saddam Hussein's weapons of mass destruction?

Halliday: I would guess, and this is purely speculation, that it's extremely modest. I think people overestimate his capacity. The military is very depleted; the equipment is very old. I fly out of Hab-

baniyah military airport. Habbaniyah is an old British base. It's lit-
tered with junked aircraft, but it also has a number of Mirage and
MIG jets, all of which are aged machinery but are flying.

So I think the capacity is largely diminished and greatly exaggerated. That's not to say it couldn't be rebuilt. Of course it could. But
as of today, I think it's of no great importance whatsoever—and certainly outgunned by the neighborhood American equipment
throughout the Gulf countries.

Q: Some people who are harshly critical of Saddam Hussein and
who take a bellicose stand say that the Oil for Food program wasn't
working and that Saddam Hussein was siphoning off the revenues
of the oil sales to feed the military, to feed himself, feather his nest.
What's the truth to that?

Halliday: Well, there's absolutely no truth, whatsoever. Every
penny from oil sales goes into the hands of the United Nations, into
a United Nations bank account, and is released by the United
Nations directly to the contractors—American, Russian, French,
Chinese, whatever they may be—who provide the foodstuffs, medical equipment, medical supplies. There's no possibility of funds
being siphoned off whatsoever.

Q: And what about the extent of the oil revenues? Was there enough
to meet the humanitarian needs?

Halliday: No, absolutely not. It fell short in that the funds available did not provide a balanced diet. We have been providing, under
the Security Council Resolution, a totally inadequate food basket for
the Iraqi people.

Q: How far short was it falling?

Halliday: In terms of calories it was short, but it was more seriously short in terms of proteins, basically animal proteins. And that
was only the immediate, day-to-day requirement. What is required
to deal with malnutrition of the kind we find in Iraq is a multisec-
toral approach. That means putting real money—and I'm talking
billions of dollars—into the health care situation, into the potable
water and sewage situation, into electric power production, into
domestic agricultural production, into education. All of that money
is simply not available.

Q: Would it not have been possible for the U.N. to say, "Look, you
can sell an unlimited amount of oil, but we're going to administer it
all through the U.N., just as we did with the Oil for Food program.
You can build up your infrastructure, but you can't siphon money off
to the military, because we're going to monitor every penny"?

Halliday: Yes, absolutely possible. But I think, sad to say, the Security Council was not prepared to have Iraq recover, rebuild, and rehabilitate itself.

It decided to sustain Iraq at a very modest survival level and thus focus the Oil for Food program to do no more than supplement the already tragic standard of living.

Q: Now, after the December bombing, Iraq is threatening to pull out of the Oil for Food program. Do you think it will? And what would be the consequences of that?

> *Sanctions will remain . . . only a device of the United Kingdom and the United States.*

Halliday: That's not a new threat. It's something they've wanted to do for a long time. They want to go it alone. They resent the intrusiveness. They are sick and tired of working with the United Nations. They feel that to continue to compromise with the United Nations is not in the best interest of Iraq.

Q: But you know how that's read in the United States: "He's willing to allow thousands of Iraqis to be killed."

Halliday: But the fact is, thousands are being killed right now, under U.N. auspices. We are killing 6,000 or 7,000 every month. I don't think you can do much worse than that. And at least they'll be running their own country. They'll have a sense of national pride and sovereignty intact. And despite their reservations about their own leadership, they'll do their damn best to make it work. And I think they'll get help—much more help than we may anticipate—from Arab neighbors, Islamic neighbors, and other countries throughout the world that will finally give up on sanctions. And sanctions will remain, in my view, only a device of the United Kingdom and the United States.

Q: After the Iraqi experience, what's your view of economic sanctions as a tool? And why were they legitimate against the apartheid regime of South Africa but not Saddam Hussein's Iraq?

Halliday: You've picked out the only possible example of economic sanctions having worked worldwide. I think there was a severe penalty for the people of South Africa, but I believe that they went along with this proposed program. This was part of their approach—the ANC [African National Congress] approach—to resolving the problem of apartheid and the government at the time. That is not the case in Iraq. These are innocent people who were not consulted. They are bearing the brunt of sanctions to a much greater degree than ever in South Africa, and we've seen the death and malnutrition that has resulted. I think it's a different circumstance. And I think it's a failed device. It's not putting pressure on the leadership, and it's certainly not producing the results that the Security Council had hoped for.

Q: Right now the United States government is again trying to find and fund some forces in Iraq that will overthrow Saddam Hussein. Do you think that is credible?

Halliday: Well, I think it makes no sense whatsoever, and frankly, I believe there are something like seventy to eighty different Iraqi opposition groups outside the country. Within the country, I think there are very few who are even in a position to contemplate any sort of change in government systems. I don't understand the viability of this program.

Q: There are those in conservative circles in the United States who say that the only real answer is for the United States to send in the ground troops, march to Baghdad, overthrow Saddam Hussein, and occupy the country.

Halliday: That's a total nonstarter. The American people would never accept that kind of exposure to its troops. The Iraqis would fight back, and the loss of life would be horrific. It would be another Vietnam.

Q: But the argument is, basically, "This guy is Hitler. You can't appease Hitler. You've got to take Hitler out." To what extent is the Hitler metaphor useful?

Halliday: National Socialism grew up because of the Versailles Treaty and the harshness of the conditions we placed on Germany after the First World War. The conditions that are being placed on Iraq are rather comparable, and we're getting the same kind of results. And that's very dangerous. If Saddam Hussein is gone tomorrow, the system can continue: The party is there, the military is there, his people are still there. There's not necessarily going to be a dramatic change. And because of sanctions, we are building a new generation of Iraqi leaders who are as mad as hell, who are introverted—more of the Taliban model.

Q: So what's your solution?

Halliday: I think we'd be much wiser to focus on the reality of Iraq today, work with what we've got, and get the country back on its feet. When the country is back on its feet, you may see change from within, that's the only change that is likely to last. Clearly, sanctions have strengthened the leadership. They've increased the dependence of the average person on the central government. And every time there is a threat of a military strike, Saddam Hussein's position is going to be enhanced. There is a naive sense that out of this sanctions situation a miracle of democracy will emerge. That, of course, is completely nonsensical. I think there is almost nobody left in the country who has time to think about governance. They're concerned with survival, putting food on the table, and getting their kids educated, and keeping themselves, their children, and their families alive. It's naive to think that positive change will come out of the present sanctions regime.

Q: So your policy would be to lift sanctions right away?

Halliday: Lift economic sanctions right away, but retain a series of devices to control arms manufacture and arms purchases.

Q: What should people do who are concerned about the plight of the Iraqi people?

Halliday: Well, we already have now forty-three members of Congress who have signed a letter to President Clinton, making a suggestion of separating the arms issue from the economic sanctions issue. That's the beginning. And there are others in Congress who are ready to think and listen and learn about the impact on the Iraqi people. Therefore it's up to the American voters to express their views through their electoral machinery.

Q: What kind of work are you doing now? Are you affiliating with a human-rights group or some other agency?

Halliday: No, in fact, I am unemployed. But I am independent, and I plan to stay that way, and speak out as I feel it is useful, to try to influence public opinion, to influence the decision-makers in Washington, London, and elsewhere.

V. Terrorism

Police barricades block access to the World Trade Center on February 27, 1993, the day after a bomb exploded in an underground parking garage, killing 6 in the first act of international terrorism perpetrated on U.S. soil.

Editor's Introduction

From plots devised by religious extremists to assaults by political fanatics, the United States has been a victim of numerous terrorist attacks since the end of the Cold War. International terrorists assail American targets particularly because of the United States' preeminence in world affairs and its tendency to intervene in disputes between foreign nations. In the last decade, several sites at home and abroad have been successfully targeted by terrorist groups, such as the World Trade Center in New York City (1993), the U.S. embassies in Tanzania and Kenya (1998), and the U.S.S. *Cole* at Aden, Yemen (2000). The United States has responded by aggressively pursuing the perpetrators of these attacks and bringing them to justice in American courts of law. Continuing terrorist threats come from a growing number of radical groups from around the world sponsored by individuals who are hostile to America. The four articles in Section V address the serious concerns that terrorist threats pose to U.S. national security.

"Terrorism: The 21st-Century War" by Howell Llewellyn asserts that modern warfare is not about occupying territories or overthrowing governments but about reducing whole societies to chaos through the use of computer viruses, toxic chemicals, biological pathogens, or suicide bombers carrying backpacks of explosives. The enemies of a state are not as easily identifiable as before, and therefore, bringing them to justice is more difficult than ever.

In "The Invisible Enemy," from *The Economist*, Lisa Rotz of the Centers for Disease Control and Prevention explains that terrorists "are often driven by hatred of particular countries, cultures, or religions." According to Rotz, in a free society like the U.S. that tolerates dissent, a terrorist attack on home soil is inevitable. Rotz finds hope in the fact that such an assault can prompt a government to strengthen its response system and also argues that the threat of bioterrorism is exaggerated, since biological weapons are notoriously difficult to develop and control.

Former F.B.I. director Louis Freeh speaks about international terrorism in "President's Fiscal Year 2000 Budget." He divides international terrorists into three categories: state sponsors of terrorism (Iran, Iraq, Syria, Sudan, Libya, Cuba, and North Korea), independent terrorist organizations such as Hamas, and individual extremists such as Ramzi Ahmed Yousef and Osama bin Laden. After discussing U.S. government responses to these threats, including sanctions, military options, and law enforcement initiative, Freeh outlines terrorist plots uncovered against Americans at home and explains how the government has dealt with them.

Steven Mufson's "Overhaul of National Security Apparatus Urged" discusses the congressionally mandated commission that proposed the creation of a National Homeland Security Agency. The commission argues that "a direct attack against American citizens on American soil is likely" over the next 25 years. To prevent its occurrence, the commission recommends the installation of five undersecretaries, for Africa, Asia, Europe, the Americas, and the Near East–South Asia, to protect U.S. embassies and interests in those regions while monitoring terrorist activities.

Terrorism: The 21st-Century War[1]

By Howell D. Llewellyn
USA TODAY MAGAZINE, March 1, 2001

Welcome George W. Bush to the presidency and the 21st century. It's a new world with many corners turned at the onset of a new millennium. Among the most critical of corners is in the conduct of war.

The major changes haven't been linked with particular counts of years, whether millennia or centuries. Firing from cover was a monumental change in tactic for Western armies that arose in the mid 18th century following encounters with savages in the colonies. Armored ships and vehicles entered the picture a century later in the American Civil War. In the mid 20th century, atomic weapons intruded on the primitiveness of human fighting by initiating the use of mass destruction in international conduct.

Today, the fast pace of technological change, an increasing level of knowledge in every imaginable party and group, easy access across borders made more porous for the purpose of international trade and investment, and a rapidly increasing global population combine to shift not merely the tactics and strategies, but the very nature of war itself. The weapons of choice have become backpack bombs, computer and biological viruses, and chemicals. Military units are no longer divisions and battalions, but teams of two or 10. Terrorism is the next highest stage of war.

Armies once were needed not only to wield the weapons of war, but to occupy the land of the enemy, like the Germans occupied much of Europe for a time or the Japanese occupied China and Korea. Modern war won't involve occupation. Americans will never occupy China or Russia, and no one will occupy America. The U.S. couldn't occupy Vietnam, and NATO forces can't really occupy Kosovo, even with a mostly friendly and appreciative population. The tactic of choice is now the dramatic explosion or chemical attack that generates fear and destroys economic functions. The objective is no longer to kill or capture or bring down the government. Instead, it is to undermine, panic, hinder, or get simple revenge.

The shift to terrorism as the means of conducting war in the 21st century poses a dramatic problem for which we are still unprepared. A war by a country's armed forces can be responded to by another nation's armed forces. There is a matching of military power measured in men, weapons, and technology. How is an act of terror to be

---

1. Reprinted from *USA Today* magazine March 2001. Copyright © 2001 by the Society for the Advancement of Education.

matched? More importantly, how is it to be prevented? The best defense for the moment seems to be the errors and simple clumsiness of the terrorists themselves.

The origins of conventional war were always in governments. In the 21st century, even individuals can wage war, and the most frequent use has been by small groups, whose power is multiplied exponentially by the change in the nature of weapons. Their power also lies in the lack of a defense. Armies, no matter how well trained or equipped, can't search every truck, car, and individual entering the U.S., let alone cordon off the vast stretches of American border that are open and untended.

> *In the 21st century, even individuals can wage war.*

Most critical, on the defensive side, is that modern states cannot apply the old aphorism that "the best defense is a good offense." The enemy of the state could be any one of 5,000,000,000 individuals. The nationality, sex, color, or religion of the enemy can never be consistently known, although Muslims, Arabs, the unshaven, and others are profiled. Governments sometimes directly back terrorists, but often do not out of concern that the weapons of terrorism could be turned on them. Given the wide and increasing availability of the weapons of terrorism, the critical variable in defense is determining intent. The key ingredients in Timothy McVeigh's bombing of the Federal Building in Oklahoma City were low-tech ammonium nitrate and a rental truck. These are the weapons of modern war. What made them weapons was what was in McVeigh's mind. The U.S.S. Cole was heavily damaged and nearly sunk and 17 Americans were killed by two men in a small boat who seemed friendly until the moment of impact. What were their beliefs that compelled them to sacrifice their lives?

There has been growing attention to defense in the U.S. against terrorism over the two decades since the American embassy was seized in Tehran, Iran. Training in counterterrorism by government agencies and even commercial businesses has expanded greatly in recent years. Counterterrorism measures include the sensitive acts of infiltration, interception of mail and phone calls, and the sharing of information about the characteristics and behaviors of profiled individuals and groups.

The trends in the impact of terrorism are not heartening. A study in the *Journal of Conflict Resolution* (June 2000) by Walter Enders and Todd Sandler shows convincingly that, although the numbers of terrorist incidents have declined, those that are still occurring are even more deadly. Each incident is now much more likely to result in death or injury than those of the 1980s, more than making up for the drop in frequency. The authors also note that there has been a dramatic shift from politically based acts to religious-based terrorism. The origins of this war are not in easily identified governments and nation-states, but in group ideologies, cult beliefs, and religious dogma. Terrorists frequently target office buildings, marketplaces, and transportation facilities, shifting away from defended, secure installations.

For the new American president, the question of the nature of a defense to a new form of war for a new century is key. Should the focus of a defense strategy and budget be on conventional warfighting power, anti-ballistic missile capability, electronic warfare in space, or detecting intent and capability of groups and individuals who focus on killing of the innocent, instilling fear, and creating chaos? The forces of economy and familiarity drive governmental strategies toward technology and raw power, while the real threat and vulnerability lies in the hearts and minds of men.

The Invisible Enemy[2]

ECONOMIST, NOVEMBER 18, 2000

Has the Threat of Bioterrorism Been Overstated?

On March 20, 1995, members of the Aum Shinrikyo cult placed containers of nerve gas in five Tokyo subway cars during the morning rush hour. As many as 6,000 people were exposed to the gas, and more than 3,000 flocked to hospital emergency rooms as word of the attack leaked out. When it was over, 12 people were dead, and a handful more had sustained permanent brain damage. The Japanese authorities later learned that the cult had carried out a similar attack the previous year, resulting in seven deaths. Aum Shinrikyo turned out to be a relatively large, sophisticated and well-financed operation staffed by highly trained people studying germ and chemical warfare.

Are such attacks the shape of things to come? At a conference on infectious diseases held this month in San Diego, Lisa Rotz of the Centre for Disease Control and Prevention in Atlanta noted that today's terrorists are often driven by hatred of particular countries, cultures, or religions. This, she suggests, means they might have fewer qualms about bioterrorism than the terrorists of several decades ago, who were more interested in scoring political points and in garnering public support for their various causes.

Dr. Rotz is not alone in her belief that bioterrorism is a growing cause for concern. Earlier this year, a $2m exercise simulating the effect of a bioterrorist attack was carried out in Denver, Colorado. It revealed serious medical and organizational shortcomings, prompting Tara O'Toole of the Johns Hopkins University Centre for Civilian Biodefence Studies to warn that America is "totally unprepared" against bioterrorists. Dr. O'Toole called for extra spending of $3 billion a year to fund new diagnostic tools, vaccines and contingency plans.

Yet a closer look suggests that those most likely to engage in bioterrorism are homegrown crackpots like Aum Shinrikyo, rather than international terrorists. And while recent incidents have had serious and sometimes fatal consequences, they have hardly resulted in widespread chaos. If anything, they have prompted governments to strengthen their response systems.

Bioterrorism is not new. The Romans used dead animals to foul their enemies' water, and the bodies of infected soldiers were catapulted into besieged towns in medieval times. More recently, most big powers have experimented with germ warfare. The former Soviet Union is estimated to have had more than 60,000 people working in its biowarfare research programme at its height. In 1972 an international consortium created the Biological and Toxin Weapons Convention, which prohibited the development and stockpiling of biological materials for hostile purposes. It went into effect in 1975, when it was ratified by 140 nations. Non-ratifiers include Libya, Iran, Iraq, and North Korea.

The Poor Man's Weapon

But new laboratory techniques mean that for about a dollar, say some analysts, a microbiologist can now generate enough material to harm people and livestock covering a square kilometre, earning bioterrorism the nickname of "the poor man's atomic bomb." The Tokyo subway incident seems to show that almost anybody can gain access to biological weapons of mass destruction.

> *The Tokyo subway incident seems to show that almost anybody can gain access to biological weapons of mass destruction.*

To Milton Leitenberg of the Centre for International and Security Studies at the University of Maryland, Baltimore, however, it proves just the opposite: that the threat of bioterrorism has been wildly exaggerated. In a recent paper, Dr. Leitenberg studied around 1,000 threatened or actual uses of bioterrorism, including hoaxes. He concluded that "there is an extremely low incidence of real biological events, in contrast to the number of recent hoaxes, the latter spawned by administrative and media hype."

According to Dr. Leitenberg, a would-be bioterrorist must be able to identify and obtain the correct pathogenic strains; handle them correctly; grow them in an environment that encourages production of the desired characteristics; store them and scale up production properly; and "weaponise" or disperse them effectively. Conventional wisdom holds that all but the fifth step are easy to accomplish, but Dr. Leitenberg says that experience shows otherwise.

Minor variations in culturing conditions can degrade an organism's toxic potential. Even in the best of circumstances it is hard to get microbes to produce toxin consistently from one generation to the next. And the most reliable way to ensure a large number of casualties is to release an inhalable aerosol over a wide area, but the technology for doing this is out of the reach of all but the most sophisticated and well-funded terrorists. Indeed, a cynic might conclude that most nations abandoned their biowarfare research because it was simply not paying off.

Dr. Leitenberg also asserts that, of the 60,000 people working in the Soviet biowarfare programme, only about 591 were senior-level scientists, and perhaps only 100 knew all the steps required to produce a biological weapon. To those who worry that these too will sell their services to the highest bidder, he points out that Aum Shinrikyo spent several million dollars trying to buy technology and expertise from former Soviet scientists, only to come away empty-handed. He concludes that most discussions on bioterrorism have been characterized by rhetoric that is "thoughtless, ill-considered, counterproductive and extravagant."

Martin Hugh-Jones, an epidemiologist at Louisiana State University in Baton Rouge, agrees that bioterrorism poses at most only a modest risk. He describes a hypothetical scenario in which a suitcase programmed to release anthrax is placed in Grand Central Station in New York during the rush hour. Victims who developed any symptoms at all would, he says, ascribe them to a mild case of the flu, rather than a terrorist attack.

In fact, biological weapons may prove more of a threat to their makers than to their intended victims. In 1979 a weaponised strain of anthrax being developed by Soviet researchers in the city of Sverdlosk was accidentally released, killing about 70 people and some livestock. Those affected all lived and worked within a narrow zone extending from the city's military facility to its southernmost limits some 30 miles away. The Soviet authorities initially insisted that people had become ill from eating tainted meat. Only in 1992 did President Yeltsin confirm the real source of the outbreak.

Dr. Hugh-Jones believes that the food supply makes a better bioterrorist target than people. An outbreak of anthrax in Kansan cattle could devastate not only American beef farmers but their suppliers and customers—grain farmers and supermarkets—as well. Or imagine if corn or wheat was infected, either with an agent that kills it, or with a disease deadly to humans, such as botulism. The result would be food scares and soaring prices. These scenarios, Dr. Hugh-Jones contends, are "far more frightening than killing a few New Yorkers." Agricultural bioterrorism is also efficient: it would take only a small outbreak of, say, kamal bunt, a wheat disease, before foreign countries started to ban imports.

It is not just terrorists who might wield such weapons: so might rival wheat producers. The American government takes this threat so seriously that in September it announced plans to spend $215m upgrading the national agricultural quarantine station on Plum

Island, off the coast of New York, to deal with threats to American agriculture. A shrewd bioterrorist, it seems, would strike where it really hurts: in the wallet.

From Statement for the Record of Louis J. Freeh, Director, Federal Bureau of Investigation, on President's Fiscal Year 2000 Budget[3]

BY LOUIS J. FREEH
WWW.FBI.GOV, FEBRUARY 4, 1999

Good morning, Mr. Chairman and members of the Subcommittee. I am pleased to have this opportunity to join Attorney General Reno and Secretary of State Albright in discussing the threat to the United States posed by terrorists both abroad and at home. . . .

The International Terrorist Situation

The current international terrorist threat can be divided into three general categories that represent a serious and distinct threat to the United States. These categories also reflect, to a large degree, how terrorists have adapted their tactics since the 1970's by learning from past successes and failures, from becoming familiar with law enforcement capabilities and tactics, and from exploiting technologies and weapons that are increasingly available to them in the post–Cold War era.

The first threat category, state sponsors of terrorism, violates every convention of international law. State sponsors of terrorism currently designated by the Department of State are: Iran, Iraq, Syria, Sudan, Libya, Cuba, and North Korea. Put simply, these nations view terrorism as a tool of foreign policy. In recent years, the terrorist activities of Cuba and North Korea appear to have declined as the economies of these countries have deteriorated. However, the terrorist activities of the other states I mentioned continue, and in some cases, have intensified during the past several years.

The second category of the international terrorist threat is represented by more formal terrorist organizations. These autonomous, generally transnational, organizations have their own infrastructures, personnel, financial arrangements, and training facilities.

---

3. Article by Louis J. Freeh from Federal Bureau of Investigation February 4, 1999. Copyright © Federal Bureau of Investigation. Reprinted with permission.

These organizations are able to plan and mount terrorist campaigns on an international basis and actively support terrorist activities in the United States.

Extremist groups such as Lebanese Hizballah, the Egyptian Al-Gama' Al-Islamiyya, and the Palestinian Hamas have supporters in the United States who could be used to support an act of terrorism here. Hizballah ranks among the most menacing of these groups. It has staged many anti-American attacks in other countries, such as the 1983 truck bombings of the United States Embassy and the United States Marine Corps barracks in Beirut, the 1984 bombing of the United States Embassy Annex in Beirut, and the 1985 hijacking of TWA Flight 847 during which United States Navy diver Robert Stehem, a passenger on the flight, was murdered by the hijackers. Elements of Hizballah were also responsible for the kidnaping and detention of United States hostages in Lebanon throughout the 1980's.

The activities of American cells of Hizballah, Hamas, and Al Gama' Al-Islamiyya generally revolve around fund-raising and low-level intelligence gathering. In addition, there are still significant numbers of Iranian students attending United States universities and technical institutions. A significant number of these students are hardcore members of the pro-Iranian student organization known as the Anjoman Islamie, which is comprised almost exclusively of fanatical, anti-American, Iranian Shiite Muslims. The Iranian Government relies heavily upon these students studying in the United States for low-level intelligence and technical expertise. However, the Anjoman Islamie also represents a significant resource base upon which the government of Iran can draw to maintain the capability to mount operations against the United States, if it so decides.

The third category of international terrorist threat stems from loosely affiliated extremists, characterized by rogue terrorists such as Ramzi Ahmed Yousef and international terrorist financier Usama bin Laden. These loosely affiliated extremists may pose the most urgent threat to the United States because these individuals bring together groups on an ad hoc, temporary basis. By not being encumbered with the demands associated with maintaining a rigid, organizational infrastructure, these individuals are more difficult for law enforcement to track and infiltrate. Individuals such as Ramzi Yousef and Usama bin Laden have also demonstrated an ability to exploit mobility and technology to avoid detection and to conduct terrorist acts. Fortunately, in 1995, we were able to capture Yousef and return him to the United States to stand trial for the

February 1993 bombing of the World Trade Center and the conspiracy to attack American aircraft overseas. Yousef was convicted in two trials and sentenced to life imprisonment.

The FBI believes that the threat posed by international terrorists in each of these categories will continue for the foreseeable future. As attention remains focused on Usama bin Laden in the aftermath of the East African bombings, I believe it is important to remember that rogue terrorists such as bin Laden represent just one type of threat that the United States faces. It is imperative that we maintain our capabilities to counter the broad range of international terrorist threats that confront the United States.

For many of us in this room, the threat of international terrorism was literally brought home by the World Trade Center bombing in February 1993. Although the plotters failed in their attempt to top-

> *It is imperative that we maintain our capabilities to counter the broad range of international terrorist threats that confront the United States.*

ple one of the twin towers into the other, an outcome that would have produced thousands of casualties, they succeeded in causing millions of dollars worth of damage in a blast that killed 6 persons and injured more than 1,000. After his capture in 1995, Ramzi Yousef, the convicted mastermind behind the New York City bombing and other terrorist acts, conceded to investigators that a lack of funding forced his group's hand in plotting the destruction of the World Trade Center. Running short of money, the plotters could not assemble a bomb as large as they had originally intended. The timing of the attack was also rushed by a lack of finances. Incredibly, the plotters' desire to recoup the deposit fee on the rental truck used to transport the bomb helped lead investigators to them. As horrible as that act was, it could very well have been much more devastating.

We are fortunate that in the nearly six years since the World Trade Center bombing, no significant act of foreign-directed terrorism has occurred on American soil. At the same time, however, we have witnessed a pattern of terrorist attacks that are either directed at United States interests or initiated in response to United States Government policies and actions. Among these acts are:

- the 1993 murders of two Central Intelligence Agency employees and the wounding of several others by Mir Amal Kasi in Langley, Virginia;

- the March 1995 attack against three employees of the United States consulate in Karachi, Pakistan, which resulted in the deaths of two Americans;

- the July 1995 hostage taking of four western tourists, including an American, by terrorists in Kashmiri, India;

- the plot by Shayk Omar Abdel Rahman and his followers to bomb several New York City landmarks, including the United Nations building, the Holland and Lincoln Tunnels, and federal buildings;

- the November 1995 bombing of a Saudi Arabian National Guard building in Riyadh, Saudi Arabia, which resulted in the deaths of five United States citizens assigned to the United States military training mission to Saudi Arabia;

- the June 1996 bombing at the Al-Khobar Towers, Dhahran, Saudi Arabia, which resulted in the deaths of 19 United States servicemen and the injury of 240 other military personnel and dependents;

- a plot led by Ramzi Yousef to destroy numerous United States air carriers in a simultaneous operation;

- a plot, also led by Ramzi Yousef, to kidnap and kill United States diplomats and foreign officials in Pakistan;

- the November 1997 ambush and massacre of foreign tourists in Luxor, Egypt, which appears to have been undertaken to pressure the United States Government to release Shayk Rahman from federal prison;

- the November 1997 murder of four United States businessmen and their driver in Karachi, Pakistan, believed to be in retaliation against the FBI's capture and rendition of Mir Amal Kasi;

- the kidnaping of seven Americans during 1998 in Colombia by terrorists groups, bringing to 92 the total number of United States citizens reported kidnaped in that country between 1980 and 1998, of which 12 Americans have died in captivity; and

- the December 1998 kidnaping of a group of western tourists, including two Americans, by terrorists in Yemen, during which four hostages were killed and one American hostage wounded when Yemeni security forces attempted a rescue operation.

As these examples illustrate, the threat of terrorism is real both at home and abroad. Usama bin Laden readily acknowledges trying to obtain chemical and biological weapons for use in his jihad, or holy war, against the United States. We also know that domestic terrorist groups have also expressed interest in chemical and biological agents. The willingness of terrorists to carry out more large-scale incidents designed for maximum destruction places a larger proportion of our population at risk. Today, Americans engaged in activities as routine as working in an office building, commuting to and from work, or visiting museums and historical sites in foreign lands, can become random victims in a deadly game acted out by international terrorists. America's democratic tradition and global presence make United States citizens and interests targets for opportunists who are willing to shed the blood of innocents for their causes.

Responding to the Threat of International Terrorism

The United States is one of the most visible and effective forces in identifying, locating, and apprehending terrorists on American soil and overseas.

The United States has developed a strong response to international terrorism. Legislation and Executive Orders enacted over the past 15 years have strengthened the ability of the United States Government to protect its citizens through five affirmative ways: diplomacy, sanctions, covert operations, military options, and law enforcement actions. For this, the Congress and the Executive Branch deserve the gratitude of the American people. We cannot accurately gauge how many potential strikes our government's strong stand against terrorism has discouraged. We can, however, measure with considerable satisfaction the success we have had in preventing plots detected in the planning stages and our successes in investigating, locating, apprehending, and prosecuting individuals who have carried out terrorist activities. I would like to highlight two aspects of this response, renditions and fund raising, that demonstrate the commitment of the United States Government to combating terrorism.

During the past decade, the United States has successfully obtained custody of 13 suspected international terrorists from foreign countries to stand trial in the United States for acts or planned acts of terrorism against our citizens. Based on its policy of treating terrorists as criminals and applying the rule of law against them, the United States is one of the most visible and effective forces in identifying, locating, and apprehending terrorists on American soil and overseas. The majority of terrorist renditions have been accomplished with the cooperation of the foreign government in which the terrorist suspect was located. Among the individuals recently returned to the United States by this process have been Mir Amal Kasi, who shot and killed two Central Intelligence Agency employees in Langley, Virginia, in 1993, and who was rendered from

Afghanistan to the United States in 1997, and Tsutomo Shirosaki, a Japanese Red Army member, who was rendered to the United States in 1996, more than 10 years after firing rockets at the United States Diplomatic Compound in Jakarta, Indonesia. Every time the United States obtains custody of a terrorist for trial, we send a clear message to terrorists everywhere that no matter how long it takes, no matter the difficulty, we will find you and you will be held accountable for your actions.

During Fiscal Year 1998, FBI investigative actions prevented 10 planned terrorist acts. Nine acts were prevented with the arrest of six members of an Illinois-based white supremacist group who were planning to target the Southern Poverty Law Center and its founder, Morris Dees; the Simon Weisenthal Center; and the New York City office of the Anti-Defamation League of B'nai B'rith. This group had also discussed robbing an armored car using a LAW rocket; poisoning the water supply of East St. Louis, Illinois; and committing several murders, including a homosexual man, a black female attorney, a member of another white supremacist group who had made derogatory comments about the Aryan Nations, and a former member of their own group. The arrest of Byron Bazarte in August 1998 prevented the bombing of an unspecified target in Washington, D.C.

Using the authorities provided under Section 302 of the Anti-Terrorism and Effective Death Penalty Act of 1996, the Secretary of State, in consultation with the Attorney General and the Secretary of the Treasury, has designated 30 groups as foreign terrorist organizations. This designation allows the United States Government to take actions to block the transfer of funds in the United States in which these organizations have an interest. The FBI provided information concerning various organizations to the Department of State to assist it in compiling the list of foreign terrorist organizations. Consistent with provisions of the Act, the FBI did not make recommendations concerning which groups should be designated as foreign terrorist organizations.

In July 1998, the FBI arrested Mawzi Mustapha Assi, a procurement agent for a foreign terrorist organization, in Dearborn, Michigan, on criminal charges relating to providing material support to a foreign terrorist organization, export of materials on the munitions control list, and other export violations. The FBI and the United States Customs Service seized $124,000 worth of sensitive night vision and navigational devices. Assi became a fugitive after the Government's unsuccessful attempts to detain him prior to trial.

We believe these provisions provide law enforcement with a potentially powerful tool to disrupt the ability of terrorist organizations to fund their destructive activities. Investigations into the financial operations of clandestine organizations on the shadowy fringes of international politics can be particularly complex, time consuming, and labor intensive. Organizations have demonstrated an ability to reinvent themselves with new names in an effort to thwart law enforcement efforts. As with measures of this type, its most powerful impact may be from its deterrent effect. As investigators and prosecutors build successful cases and precedents to enforce anti-fund raising activities, targeted groups may decide that fund raising in the United States is too difficult and risky.

The Domestic Terrorism Threat

Domestic terrorist groups are those which are based and which operate entirely within the United States, or its territories, and whose activities are directed at elements of the United States Government or its civilian population. Domestic terrorist groups represent interests that span the full political spectrum, as well as social issues and concerns. FBI investigations of domestic terrorist groups or individuals are not predicated upon social or political beliefs; rather, they are based upon planned or actual criminal activity. The current domestic terrorist threat primarily comes from right-wing extremist groups, Puerto Rican extremist groups, and special interest extremists.

Right-wing Extremist Groups

The threat from right-wing extremist groups includes militias, white-separatist groups, and anti-government groups. All right-wing extremist groups tend to encourage massing weapons, ammunition and supplies in preparation for a confrontation with federal law enforcement, as well as local law enforcement who are often perceived as agents for the State/Federal government.

The goal of the militia movement is to defend and protect the United States Constitution from those who want to take away the rights of Americans. The militia movement believes that the United States Constitution gives Americans the right to live their lives without government interference. The FBI is not concerned with every single aspect of the militia movement since many militia members are law-abiding citizens who do not pose a threat of violence. The FBI focuses on radical elements of the militia movement capable and willing to commit violence against government, law enforcement, civilian, military and international targets (U.N., visiting foreign military personnel). Not every state in the union has a militia problem. Militia activity varies from states with almost no militia activity (Hawaii, Connecticut) to states with thousands of active militia members (Michigan, Texas).

The American militia movement has grown over the last decade. Factors contributing to growth include:

- **Guns**—The right to bear arms is an issue [on] which almost all militia members agree and most militia members believe a conspiracy exists to take away their guns. The national system of instant background checks for all gun buyers, mandated by the 1993 Brady Act and which actually was implemented on November 30, 1998, has further angered many militia groups. These militia members see this new law as another example of how the government is conspiring to take away their guns. The banning of semiautomatic assault weapons has also angered many militia members.

- **State Laws**—Militias resent state laws forbidding them to gather together to fire weapons. Sixteen states have laws which prohibit all militia groups and 17 states have laws which prohibit all paramilitary training.

- **Mistrust of Federal Law Enforcement** is frequently mentioned in militia literature and overall militia mythology. FBI and Bureau of Alcohol, Tobacco and Firearms (ATF) actions, such as Ruby Ridge, the Branch Davidians, and the Freeman standoff, are cited, and thus [these organizations] are hated and distrusted by many militia members.

- **Taxes**—Militia members believe that they pay too many taxes and that those tax dollars are wasted by a huge, uncaring and inefficient bureaucracy in Washington, D.C. Since the Internal Revenue Service collects federal taxes, it is widely hated by militia members.

- **The United Nations** is perceived as an organization bent on taking over the world and destroying American democracy and establishing "the New World Order." The New World Order theory holds that, one day, the United Nations will lead a military coup against the nations of the world to form a one-world government. United Nations troops, consisting of foreign armies, will commence a military takeover of America. The United Nations will mainly use foreign troops on American soil because foreigners will have fewer reservations about killing American citizens. Captured United States military bases will be used to help conquer the rest of the world.

Most of the militia movement has no racial overtones and does not espouse bigotry; there are some black and Jewish militia members. However, the pseudo-religion of Christian Identity, as well as other hate philosophies, have begun to creep into the militia movement. This scenario is currently being played out in the Michigan Militia, arguably the largest militia group in America. Lynn Van Huizen, leader of the Michigan Militia Corps, is currently trying to oust Christian Identity factions from his group. Christian Identity is a belief system that provides both a religious base for racism and anti-Semitism, and an ideological rationale for violence against minorities. This pattern of racist elements seeping into the militia movement is a disturbing trend, as it will only strengthen the radical elements of the militias.

Overhaul of National Security Apparatus Urged[4]

By Steven Mufson
Washington Post, February 1, 2001

Citing U.S. vulnerability to terrorist attacks, porous borders and new technologies, a congressionally mandated commission on national security yesterday recommended the creation of a National Homeland Security Agency, sharply higher spending on scientific research and education, and an overhaul of government institutions.

The U.S. Commission on National Security, led by former senators Gary Hart (D-Colo.) and Warren B. Rudman (R-N.H.), warned that "without significant reforms, American power and influence cannot be sustained." It offered the most far-reaching blueprint for reforming the national security apparatus since a similar effort in 1947.

The report comes as the Bush administration is in the midst of reexamining the government's foreign policy institutions. Defense Secretary Donald H. Rumsfeld is turning to new threats, Secretary of State Colin L. Powell is trying to reenergize the foreign service, and national security adviser Condoleezza Rice is trimming the size and altering the role of the National Security Council.

Rudman said members of the study group will meet with Powell on Friday and plan meetings with other top administration officials to discuss the recommendations.

The commission's proposals include unifying the Coast Guard, the Customs Service, the Federal Emergency Management Agency and the Border Patrol into the new homeland security body, whose director would have Cabinet status.

The new agency would coordinate defense against attacks as well as responses if an attack succeeded. The main task of the National Guard would be changed to deal with the prospect of an attack on U.S. soil.

"It is unlikely that we will continue to be the blessed country we've been all these years," Rudman said, referring to the possibility of an attack by a foreign power. "The threat is asymmetric and we're not prepared for it."

The report also suggested doubling federal funds for science and technology research by 2010, abolishing the National Economic Council, reducing the staff and role of the National Security Council, streamlining the Pentagon, merging authorizing and appropriations committees in Congress, and radically altering the structure of the State Department.

Members of the commission acknowledged that implementing its recommendations would be difficult, noting that many previous departmental reorganization reports were shelved.

"We put down what we thought ought to be done," Rudman said. "Just because it's difficult doesn't mean it's impossible."

> *"A direct attack against American citizens on American soil is likely over the next quarter century."*—U.S. Commission on National Security

The commission's most pressing language was aimed at international terrorism. "A direct attack against American citizens on American soil is likely over the next quarter century," the group said.

That seems to reflect a growing fear among policymakers at a time when the gap between the traditional war-fighting abilities of the United States and other nations has widened significantly.

Many of the report's suggestions focused on the State Department, which the group called a "crippled institution, starved for resources by Congress because of its inadequacies" and a "demoralized and relatively ineffective body." The group said the department "rarely speaks with one voice, thus reducing its influence and credibility in its interactions with the Congress and in its representation abroad." And the commission added that many of the department's "core functions were parceled out to other agencies."

To deal with a changing world, the commission suggested creating five undersecretaries for Africa, Asia, Europe, the Americas, and the Near East–South Asia, and redefining the responsibilities of the undersecretary for global affairs.

The position of undersecretary for political affairs would be abolished, but the undersecretary for management would be retained. Each regional undersecretary would deal with three major subcategories: economic and transnational issues, political affairs, and security matters.

The commission also was sharply critical of the Defense Department, where it said that the growth in staff had "created mounting confusion and delay." It suggested the Defense Department reduce its infrastructure costs by 20 to 25 percent over 10 years by outsourcing as many support activities as possible.

The group also said the Pentagon should change its acquisition procedures to make them less bureaucratic and better suited to long-range planning. "The weapons acquisition process is so hobbled by excessive laws, regulations and oversight strictures that it can neither recognize nor seize opportunities for major innovation," the report said.

The National Security Council, the report continued, had assumed policymaking roles that it was never intended to have. The commission report said it should return to the much-needed role of policy coordinator.

"The NSC adviser should keep a low public profile," the report said.

The Bush administration has already reduced the profile of Rice, the national security adviser, by making her position a non-Cabinet-level post.

In addition to Rudman and Hart, the commission included former House speaker Newt Gingrich (R-Ga.); lawyer and former commerce undersecretary Lionel H. Olmer; former representative Lee H. Hamilton (D-Ind.), director of the Woodrow Wilson International Center; business executive and former Air Force secretary Donald B. Rice; Norman R. Augustine, chairman of Lockheed Martin Corp.'s executive committee; Anne Armstrong, a Nixon and Ford administration official and former ambassador to Britain; John R. Galvin, former supreme allied commander for Europe; Council on Foreign Relations President Leslie H. Gelb; former NBC diplomatic correspondent John Dancy; James R. Schlesinger, a former energy and defense secretary and CIA director; former U.N. ambassador Andrew Young; and retired Adm. Harry D. Train.

VI. Spies Like Us . . . and Them

This photograph shows the "Ellis" drop site under a bridge over Wolftrap Creek at Foxstone Park in Vienna, Va., where former F.B.I. agent Robert Hanssen left documents containing U.S. government secrets for his Russian contacts during a 15-year espionage operation.

Editor's Introduction

Though most capitalist and communist nations engaged in espionage to some degree during the Cold War, the U.S. and the Soviet Union dominated the spy trade. The superpowers used espionage to gain an advantage in the event of an armed conflict, to frustrate one another's plans, and to advance their own agendas. Though the Cold War ended in 1991, spying continued on both sides, as we see with the recent case of F.B.I. Special Agent Robert Hanssen, who sold secrets to the Russians for 15 years until his capture in 2001. The articles in Section VI explore post–Cold War espionage activity, including the consequences of getting caught, the Hanssen case, and plans for a Cold War museum in Washington, D.C.

The section begins with two articles about two spies, one working for the United States against the Soviet Union and the other working for the Soviets and, later, the Russians against the U.S. David Pryce-Jones reports in "In From the Cold War" on the 1992 defection of former K.G.B. agent Vasili Nikitich Mitrokhin, who, while spying on the Soviet Union for the C.I.A., collected trunkloads of documents detailing Soviet attempts to recruit American scientists and politicians to sabotage U.S. national security. "Invisible on the Inside" by Vernon Loeb and Walter Pincus then details Hanssen's career as a Russian spy and explores his motivation for betraying his country. Steven Ashley's "Rules of Espionage: Got Caught? You Lose Players" discusses an ironclad rule of spying, that when one nation catches another nation's spy, that other nation must forfeit some of its diplomatic corps. Hence, when Hanssen was caught spying on the U.S. for Russia, 50 Russian diplomats were expelled from the U.S., with Russia threatening a similar move against U.S. diplomats in retaliation.

The American people may have exhaled a collective sigh of relief at the apparent end of the Cold War in the 1990s, but as several articles in this section indicate, U.S. relations with former and current communist rivals remain chilly. Robin Wright reports on the problematic state of Russian-American relations in "East-West Mistrust Hasn't Crumbled, as Arrest Shows," while Keay Davidson presents expert opinions on the extent to which the American government should trust (or mistrust) China in "Spying on China Is Essential to U.S. Security, Analysts Agree." An excerpt from a *Mechanical Engineering* article, "Palm-Size Spy Plane," next describes the development of miniature spy planes designed to search "small-area" terrain, such as industrial facilities and military complexes. In the final article, "These Days, the Cold War Is Getting a Warm Reception," Phil Patton looks at the Cold War Museum planned in Washington, which will display spy-related materials, such as an American U-2 plane and a Soviet KH-11 satellite, along with a fallout shelter and a piece of the Berlin Wall. A list of espionage cases from the last 30 years is also included in this section.

In From the Cold War: The Latest From the KGB[1]

By David Pryce-Jones
National Review, October 11, 1999

Communism had just gone belly up when early in 1992 Vasili Nikitich Mitrokhin caught a train from Moscow to an unnamed Baltic capital—Riga in Latvia, by the sound of it. There he contacted the CIA. A trusted member of the KGB since 1948, he had been one of its senior archivists for more than a decade, with unrestricted access to its files. You might think that our Vasili would have been recognized, and welcomed, as a defector. He, if anyone, knew the KGB's inside story, and he had the documents to tell it. But the CIA geniuses had no time for Mitrokhin. Over the years, the United States had been penetrated by Soviet espionage and subversion at every level, but the CIA no longer felt the need to know. Only a short while before, the Agency had been predicting that by the year 2000 the Soviet Union would have a larger economy than the United States.

So Mitrokhin walked down the road to the British. For decades, Soviet agents had displayed a professionalism against which the British appeared defenseless. Now, at least, the British delivered Mitrokhin and many trunks of documents back to Britain. Exposure and prosecution of Soviet agents might have been expected. The British, though, were in a quandary. Mitrokhin's files were copies, and so might not satisfy the rules of evidence in court. This allowed the grateful secret services to exercise their one real skill of sweeping as much as possible under the carpet, but they nevertheless came to an unusual deal. Mitrokhin was to collaborate with Christopher Andrew, professor of modern history at Cambridge and a well-known expert on the KGB, to publish what the authorities would permit.

What Mitrokhin managed to copy and squirrel away reveals only a small part of the KGB effort internationally, but it is enough to stand as an astounding record of Communism, a commemoration of the Soviets as they really were. The archive shows that one or another department of the KGB considered how to approach, to monitor, or, at best, to recruit everyone who was anyone politically in the United States and Europe throughout the postwar period.

---

1. Copyright © 1999 by *National Review*, Inc. 215 Lexington Avenue, New York, NY 10016. Reprinted by permission.

Many of these schemes were ridiculous, of course, but the KGB did succeed in assembling a slew of renegade politicians and parliamentarians, civil servants and academics, and opinion-formers in the media, especially the left-wing press.

One significant success was to compromise Willy Brandt, the West German chancellor, in a way that led to his resignation. British prime minister Harold Wilson earned himself a code name in the files by shooting his mouth off indiscreetly and often to someone he knew to be a KGB agent. Approaches were made to men as varied as Cyrus Vance and Oskar Lafontaine, the German socialist. In 1975 alone, KGB head Yuri Andropov typically ordered operations to penetrate the "inner circles" of George Ball, Ramsey Clark, Averell Harriman, Edward Kennedy, Theodore Sorensen, and others. Plans existed for the murder of a range of personalities, from Marshal Tito in Yugoslavia to Soviet defectors, especially those from the KGB itself. Rudolf Nureyev and Natalia Makarova both escaped the Soviet Union to dance abroad, and their legs were to be broken as fitting punishment. Bomb attacks were arranged in black districts of New York, with the blame laid on the Jewish Defense League. Sexual smears were invented about Senator Scoop Jackson, Martin Luther King, and J. Edgar Hoover. The AIDS virus, the KGB put about, had been "manufactured" in Maryland.

Thanks to the number of agents operating in U.S. defense laboratories, American science effectively became Soviet science. Secret arms caches and radio transmitters, we now learn, were buried in a dozen countries (including America, Turkey, and Israel) for the day when war was openly declared and sabotage behind the lines could begin.

Only weeks ago, researchers happen to have discovered the names of British agents working for the Stasi, the East German secret police. Almost daily, some figures who were always suspected and others who were unknown are being exposed as traitors. It would all be as laughable as a French farce about mistaken identities, except that fundamental questions of security and justice are at stake.

An institutional imagination was at work. The KGB sought and found people who fantasized about the Soviet Union, the huge majority of them deceiving themselves for psychological reasons, living in an illusory dream quite distinct from reality. Like some compulsive seducer, the KGB operated on the principle that you should take every chance, because you could never know your luck, and even clever people were often the fantasizers they wanted.

Remember "Reds under the beds"? Remember how anyone who worried that Communist agents and spies might be undermining the democracies met the reflex sneer "McCarthyite"? The revelation that Reds had more nearly occupied every room in the house has not yet been enough to prompt anyone to apologize. As for those exposed now in the Mitrokhin-Andrew and Stasi archives, either they are defiant or they prevaricate. Brought to confront the reality that they had voluntarily engaged in a world-wide net of blackmail, sexual entrapment, forgery, and lying, they prefer to retreat into more fantasizing about the Soviet Union and of Communism. The self-deception is altogether a central phenomenon of this age.

Treason and spying now pass as facts of life about which nothing can be done, if the outstanding example of Melita Norwood is anything to go by. Mitrokhin provided the information. The daughter of an emigre Latvian Communist, Norwood became a full Soviet agent in 1937, at the height of Stalin's terror. Her job as a secretary at the British Non-Ferrous Metals Research Association allowed her

---

Treason and spying now pass as facts of life about which nothing can be done.

---

access to the development of the atomic bomb. By the time anyone thought of vetting her in the early Fifties, she had passed this institute's research on to the Soviets. Only a specialist can determine the damage she did, but the Rosenbergs were executed for comparable treachery. Recently two senior Chinese officers were put to death for passing military secrets to Taiwan. Britain still has capital punishment for treason.

Melita Norwood lives in Bexleyheath, a cozy suburb of south London. Aged 87, and outwardly a dear old grandmother with pink cheeks and a woolly cardigan, she is in a time warp of pure revolutionary illusion. Communism, she says, was about giving "ordinary people food and fares they could afford, good education and a health service"—a reasonable description of surrounding Bexleyheath. "I loved Lenin. But old Joe, well, he didn't turn out so good. He wasn't a hundred percent." To one journalist who interviewed her, the lack of a sense of guilt at her treason was "spellbinding." It was her duty to help Russia, she says, and she'd do it all over again. As for Mitrokhin, "As a good pacifist, I could shoot him. What about the effect on the people he is exposing?"

Comically absurd as she may sound, she knows that the secret services have known about her since Mitrokhin defected in 1992. They have not even made contact with her, she boasts. She is daring them to take her to court, safe in the well-founded belief that they will do no such thing. Harassing pink-cheeked grannies isn't nice, is it, and besides it was a long time ago, there isn't a Soviet Union any more, and who cares?

There isn't a Nazi Germany either, but not long ago a law was passed in Britain to prosecute Nazi war crimes retrospectively. The objection that such crimes were committed outside British jurisdiction by people not responsible to British law was summarily overridden. Under this recent law, Anton Gekas, Szymon Serafimowicz, and Andrzej Sawoniuk have been brought to trial, and a great deal of trouble was taken to establish exactly what these three elderly grandfathers did or did not do for the Nazi cause, with life imprisonment duly handed down as a sentence.

Augusto Pinochet arrived in Britain as a guest of the Ministry of Defense a year ago. In 1973 he had staged a military coup against Salvador Allende, a Moscow loyalist, and taken power himself in Chile. Undoubtedly he persecuted Communists, and in return the Soviet Union switched its propaganda machine up to full throttle to establish him as a Nazi-type dictator, a prime hate figure. Stepping down of his own free will, Pinochet left his country stable and democratic. He is now 83, and a grandfather. A self-declared left-wing Spanish magistrate took advantage of Pinochet's visit to serve a writ on him in Britain for crimes committed under his rule in Chile. Any such crimes were outside British (and Spanish) jurisdiction, and those responsible for them are not answerable to British (or Spanish) law. Nevertheless the British government arrested Pinochet and continues to hold him under house arrest while trying to interpret, bend, or invent legal small print to justify its actions. The government appears to be about to extradite Pinochet to Spain.

Anyone categorized as a Nazi, then, whether fairly or unfairly, is brought to account, by whatever legal process can be devised. Proud holder of the Order of the Red Banner, in contrast, Mrs. Norwood enjoys being photographed amid the flowers in her front garden. The Mitrokhin-Andrew revelations are evidently a nine-day wonder, to be shrugged off without any legal or even social repercussions for anyone. The Soviet Union indeed lost the Cold War, but its revenge is a legacy of double standards, with one law for the Left, and another, quite different, for the Right.

Invisible on the Inside[2]

By Vernon Loeb and Walter Pincus
Washington Post, February 21, 2001

On Oct. 4, 1985, a KGB officer received a letter at his home in Alexandria. Inside was a second envelope with the warning: "DO NOT OPEN. TAKE THIS ENVELOPE UNOPENED TO VICTOR I. CHERKASHIN."

According to court documents made public yesterday, the letter was sent by FBI Special Agent Robert P. Hanssen and contained an anonymous offer to hand over some of the U.S. government's most sensitive secrets in return for cash.

But from the start, Hanssen was no ordinary "walk-in" spy. He allegedly took elaborate precautions to keep his identity a secret, even from the Russians, and chose his initial handler in Cherkashin, a top KGB officer whom he admired professionally.

That kind of caution and inside knowledge, U.S. officials said, are what allowed Hanssen to operate as a mole for 15 years—longer even than the CIA's Aldrich Ames, who was caught in 1994 after nine years as a spy.

Thus, Hanssen proved what counterintelligence experts at the FBI and CIA have long known and feared: that a trusted agent working for one side can spy for the other as long as he is smart, careful and not too greedy.

Add to that what some experts consider pervasive security flaws in the U.S. intelligence community—such as widespread access to computers with top-secret information and a lack of random polygraphing at the FBI—and the results, in the words of FBI Director Louis J. Freeh, are "exceptionally grave."

At a somber news conference yesterday, Freeh said Hanssen evaded detection for so long because he was "a very, very experienced intelligence officer"—so disciplined, Freeh maintained, that Hanssen's Russian controllers learned his real name only when the FBI announced his arrest.

"My identity and actual position," Hanssen allegedly told the KGB in his very first letter, "must be left unstated to ensure my security."

Even as he moved up the FBI's career ladder into ever more sensitive positions that gave him astonishingly broad access to counterintelligence information, according to a 109-page FBI affidavit filed in

---

Three Decades of Espionage Cases

David H. Barnett was a CIA officer who sold information about the organization's undercover operations to the Soviet Union. Between 1976 and 1977, Barnett earned $92,000 from the KGB for providing U.S. intelligence about the Soviet SA-2 surface-to-air missile and the Whiskey class diesel-power submarine. He pleaded guilty shortly after his arrest in 1980 and was sentenced to 18 years in prison but was paroled in 1990.

Ronald W. Pelton spied for the Soviet Union from 1980 to 1983 while working for the National Security Agency. The USSR allegedly paid him $35,000 for classified information about collection projects involving Soviet targets. Upon his arrest in 1985, Pelton pleaded not guilty but was convicted of two counts of espionage and sentenced to three life sentences.

Sharon M. Scrange was arrested in 1985 for supplying Ghanian intelligence officers with the identities of CIA agents. She complied with the FBI by providing information about her Ghanian boyfriend, **Michael Soussoudis**, who reportedly sold items of U.S. intelligence to such countries as Cuba, Libya, East Germany, and other Eastern Bloc nations. Scrange spent two years in prison, while Soussoudis's sentence of 20 years was suspended

court, Hanssen refused to meet with Soviet (or later, Russian) agents in person in Washington or abroad—knowing that those agents are often under surveillance and that foreign trips would draw suspicion.

While he allegedly pocketed $600,000 in cash and diamonds, plus $800,000 in foreign bank deposits, Hanssen did not engage in flamboyant spending. At one point, he even advised the KGB not to send him too much cash.

"I have little need or utility for more than the [$]100,000. It merely provides a difficulty since I cannot spend it, store it or invest it easily," he allegedly wrote, adding that the KGB could "perhaps [send] some diamonds as security to my children" and that "eventually, I would appreciate an escape plan."

Moreover, according to the FBI affidavit, Hanssen took numerous other precautions that only a trained counterintelligence professional would follow, such as exchanging information at arranged "dead drops," using code for dates and places, and encrypting computer diskettes. But he refused to accept KGB radio transmitters or other spy devices, which if discovered would immediately incriminate him.

Former FBI director William H. Webster, whom Freeh has asked to assess the damage resulting from Hanssen's alleged espionage, said yesterday that Hanssen knew the bureau's counterintelligence "matrix" too well.

"They keep track of anyone who has ever met or contacted a Russian," Webster said in an interview. "When someone avoids direct contact, and none is observed, there is a problem."

Nonetheless, Freeh acknowledged at his press conference that Webster's review is all but certain to find flaws in FBI procedures for ferreting out spies. One area likely to be scrutinized, according to present and former officials, is the bureau's unwillingness to give polygraph or "lie detector" tests to employees on a periodic basis.

While polygraphing of recruits began in 1993, the FBI—unlike the CIA and National Security Agency—has no agency-wide program for ongoing testing of its officers.

One former top FBI counterintelligence official said the bureau has shied away from polygraphing agents because, he said, "We consider it an inexact science." Now, he added, "They will have to look at it again."

Edward J. Curran, who as a former top FBI counterintelligence expert went to the CIA to tighten security after the Ames case, was sharply critical yesterday of the bureau's policy. "There has been a program for regular polygraphing of FBI agents waiting to be approved for three years," he said.

Freeh declined to comment on whether Hanssen had been polygraphed during his 25-year FBI career. In that time, Hanssen rose from counterintelligence officer to supervisor of a foreign counterintelligence squad, supervisory special agent-in-charge of the FBI's Soviet Analytical Unit and, finally, the bureau's chief representative at the State Department. He was recalled from that position in January after he came under suspicion.

By then, his elaborate tradecraft was for naught. While Freeh and other U.S. officials declined to discuss the source of their information, it appears that Hanssen was betrayed by a Russian source who gave his entire KGB dossier to the United States.

The FBI's affidavit quotes from dozens of alleged communications between Hanssen and the KGB or its successor agency, the Russian Foreign Intelligence Service (SVR), including postmarks on letters that Hanssen mailed to his handlers.

Indeed, according to the FBI's account, Hanssen had worried for years about being betrayed by someone from the other side.

Eleven days after his first anonymous letter to the KGB in 1985, Hanssen allegedly sent a package stuffed with classified documents through the U.S. mail to the Virginia home of a KGB officer named Viktor Degtyar—a move he later apologized for. The channel, he said, was unsecure, but he needed some means of establishing his "long-term value."

on condition he leave the U.S. within 24 hours.

Steven J. Lalas used his position at the State Department to supply Greece with U.S. military information, including 700 documents pertaining to the U.S. strategy in the Balkans. Lalas stole and sold CIA reports about troop strength, political analysis, and military discussions between the U.S. Embassy in Athens and the White House. From 1991 to 1993, Lalas was paid $20,000 for roughly 240 documents. After his arrest in 1993, he was sentenced to 14 years in prison for one count of conspiracy to commit espionage.

Aldrich Ames and his wife, **Maria Del Rosario Casa Ames,** sold classified information to the KGB and its successor, the Ministry of Security for the Russian Federation, from 1983 to 1994. During this time, 10 U.S. and Allied agents were executed, and Aldrich allegedly collected $2,500,000. The couple was arrested in 1994 after a lengthy investigation. Aldrich was sentenced to life imprisonment without parole, while Maria received five years in prison under a plea bargain.

Harold J. Nicholson, a CIA agent, earned $120,000 from the Russians over three years for information about CIA officers and foreign business people, which he stole by hacking into the agency's system. After his arrest and indictment in 1996, Nicholson pleaded guilty in 1997 and was sentenced to 23 years in prison.

Robert Hanssen, an FBI agent for 25 years, was arrested in 2001 for spying for the Russians for 15 years. Hanssen allegedly gained the trust of his Russian counterparts by expressing disdain for the U.S. government, calling it a "retarded child." Refusing to meet with Russian agents in person, he conducted his spy operation by leaving packages for his contacts at strategic drop sites in the Washington, D.C., area. He allegedly sold more than 6,000 pages of documents for $600,000 worth of diamonds and cash. There was a reported $400,000 waiting for him when he was caught. He was never suspected by his co-workers and avoided exposure by using his counterintelligence skills. Hanssen could be charged with the death penalty, since the information he sold resulted in the deaths of other FBI agents.

Sources: *www.dss.mil, cicentre.com*, and *Time.com*

It almost cost him. FBI agents observed Degtyar walking into the Soviet Embassy the next morning "carrying a large black canvas bag which he did not typically carry."

But that was the last time any secret documents went in the mail. Inside that black canvas bag, Degtyar allegedly carried Hanssen's detailed instructions about dead-drop locations, package preparation, signal locations and signaling techniques.

Three years later, Hanssen was still obsessing over tradecraft. "My security concerns may seem excessive," he wrote his handlers in July 1988, three days before allegedly turning over 530 pages of highly classified material. "I believe experience has shown them to be necessary. I am much safer if you know little about me. Neither of us are children about these things. Over time, I can cut your losses rather than become one."

Repeatedly, Hanssen refused to adopt tradecraft options suggested by his handlers, insisting they do things his way. Given what he was capable of producing, the KGB and its successor, the SVR, also expressed concern for the security of the agent they called "Ramon," or simply "B."

After Hanssen informed his handlers in May 1990 that he had been promoted to a post as a traveling member of the FBI's Headquarter's Inspections Staff, his handlers wrote back: "Congratulations on Your promotion. We wish You all the very best in Your life and career . . . So, do your new job, make Your trips, take Your time . . ."

A year later, with the Soviet Union collapsing, the KGB sent "B" a package containing $12,000 in cash as payment for his latest document delivery and a computer diskette that read in part: "We've done all in order that none of those events ever affects Your security and our ability to maintain the operation with You."

By this point, Hanssen had become intensely loyal to his handlers—"insanely loyal," he protested in a letter to the SVR in March 2000, complaining like a jilted lover when his handlers failed to respond to one of his signal marks—a piece of white adhesive tape on a sign post in Virginia.

Throughout the long spy dance, he expressed scorn for his employer and the capabilities of his colleagues, though not to the point of overconfidence.

"The U.S. can be errantly likened to a powerfully built but retarded child," he wrote the SVR in June 2000, "potentially dangerous, but young, immature and easily manipulated. But don't be fooled by that appearance. It is also one which can turn into genius quickly, like an idiot savant, once convinced of a goal."

Hanssen certainly never took the FBI lightly. More than three years ago, he began repeatedly searching the FBI's Electronic Case File computer system for any references to himself, his address and his city of residence, Vienna.

Back in November, he again refused to meet his handlers overseas, revealing the methodical approach that had protected him all these years.

"I must answer too many questions from family, friends, and government plus it is a cardinal sign of a spy," he allegedly wrote. "You have made it that way because of your policy. Policies are constraints, constraints breed patterns. Patterns are noticed."

Whether Hanssen would have been caught without being betrayed may never be known. But by the time he was betrayed, his guard was slipping, if ever so slightly.

> *"The U.S. can be errantly likened to a powerfully built but retarded child."*—
> **Robert Hanssen**

In December, when the FBI had learned about Hanssen and was carrying out surveillance on his movements, the veteran FBI counterintelligence agent made a series of mistakes that marked him as a potential spy.

On Dec. 12, he was seen driving four times past a park sign in Vienna that was used to signal whether the Russians had left something for him. That same night, he walked into a store at a nearby shopping center at a time when a known Russian intelligence officer was in front of the store.

Two weeks later, Hanssen drove by the signal site three times. One time he stopped in front of it, another time he parked and walked up to the sign, and a third time he pointed a flashlight at it. All three actions would have called attention to him, one former FBI agent said. "Recent changes in U.S. law now attach the death penalty to my help to you as you know, so I do take some risk," Hanssen allegedly said in the November letter to his handlers. "On the other hand, I know far better than most what minefields are laid . . ."

Rules of Espionage: Got Caught? You Lose Players[3]

BY JAMES RISEN
NEW YORK TIMES, MARCH 23, 2001

Retaliatory measures now under way between Washington and Moscow fit neatly into the long-established rules of the espionage game that the two sides have played by ever since their first spies went out into the cold to do silent battle.

President Bush's decision to expel four Russian diplomats immediately, and demand that the Russians withdraw 46 more by July 1, is the largest such action since 1986 and far more aggressive than any similar move taken by the United States since the collapse of the Soviet Union. Russian officials, complaining that the Bush administration is trying to return to a Cold War mentality, vowed to retaliate in kind.

But the actions follow the general rule that both the United States and the Soviet Union, and now Russia, have always accepted: when one side gets caught running a spy on the other's turf, some intelligence officers serving under cover as diplomats have to go home.

That the spy in question may have volunteered to betray his country without much persuasion from his professional handlers doesn't matter. The rule of thumb is simple: get caught and go home.

This explains why the Bush administration singled out for immediate expulsion the Russian intelligence officers whom the United States believes were directly involved in handling the case of Robert Philip Hanssen, the F.B.I. agent arrested last month on charges that he spied for Moscow for more than 15 years.

Still, another rule of the game is that there is something approaching professional courtesy in the espionage world. Intelligence officers, whether Americans from the Central Intelligence Agency or Russians from the S.V.R., successor of the K.G.B., almost never face serious harm themselves, even when they get caught red-handed.

Sometimes an intelligence officer will be arrested after the spy being handled has been unmasked. But because professional case officers almost always work under diplomatic cover and have diplomatic immunity, they are quickly released.

While the agents whom they have been handling face either long prison terms or even possible execution by their government, the worst that the foreign intelligence officers usually face is a public outing and a declaration by the opposing government that they are persona non grata, and must quickly leave.

At the end of one the most important spy operations run by the C.I.A. against the Soviets during the Cold War, for example, the Soviet scientist Adolf Tolkachev was detained in 1985. After Mr. Tolkachev's arrest and inter-

> *The rule of thumb is simple: get caught and go home.*

rogation, the K.G.B. lured a C.I.A. officer, Paul Stombaugh, to what he believed was a meeting with Mr. Tolkachev. When Mr. Stombaugh arrived at the meeting site, the K.G.B. arrested him. He was quickly released; the sole purpose of the K.G.B. ambush had been to out an American and briefly weaken the C.I.A.'s operations in Moscow.

An ironclad rule of the game is that when one side orders the expulsion of intelligence officers as a result of an espionage case, the other country orders the expulsion of a similar number of intelligence officers—even if they have not been caught in a spy case themselves. After the arrest of a C.I.A. officer, Aldrich Ames, in 1994 on charges of spying for Moscow, the Clinton administration ordered the expulsion of one Russian, the Washington station chief. In response, the Russians ordered the expulsion of the C.I.A.'s station chief in Moscow.

President Bush's move appears to have the added component of using the Hanssen case as a pretext for a broad move to reduce the Russian intelligence presence in the United States, which American officials complain has crept up to Cold War levels.

In the latter stages of the Cold War, the C.I.A. and K.G.B. even opened a regular channel of communications to make certain that the two agencies were working from the same informal playbook. With tensions running high during the Reagan administration, senior K.G.B. officials approached their C.I.A. counterparts and proposed the creation of a special communications line between the spy agencies.

After fits and starts, the "Gavrilov channel"—named by the K.G.B. after a 19th-century Russian poet—led to secret meetings between senior C.I.A. and K.G.B. officials in neutral sites like Vienna and Helsinki.

For years, "Gavrilov" meetings enabled American and Soviet intelligence officials to make sure that both the C.I.A. and the K.G.B. understood the state of play in the espionage world. Yet new realities have intruded as the Bush administration has moved against the Russians.

After the end of the Cold War, the C.I.A. and the S.V.R. began a formal relationship—a considerable expansion of "Gavrilov" style meetings—while the F.B.I. opened an office in Moscow and officials began meeting with their Russian counterparts as well. The two sides meet frequently to discuss issues on which they believe they can cooperate, like counterterrorism and counternarcotics programs.

The official liaison programs have added a new and rather awkward layer to the spy-versus-spy relationship.

Today, for instance, an American official noted that the S.V.R.'s station chief in Washington was not among those being declared persona non grata. That Russian official's position is openly declared to the United States, and he is involved in liaison relations.

Despite its expulsion order and tough words to Moscow, the Bush administration apparently believes it would be counterproductive to expel him.

In addition, American officials noted today that the C.I.A. was "a team player" in the decision to expel a large number of Russians, despite a certain reprisal against its own officers in Russia. One possible explanation is that the C.I.A. has opened stations throughout many of the former Soviet republics and in the capitals of former Warsaw Pact allies in eastern Europe, giving the agency avenues denied it during the Soviet era.

East-West Mistrust Hasn't Crumbled, as Arrest Shows[4]

By Robin Wright
Los Angeles Times, February 21, 2001

The arrest of a high-level FBI agent accused of spying for Russia for a decade after the demise of the Soviet Union reveals just how little things have changed since the Cold War.

Despite the end of an intense ideological rivalry, Moscow still runs its largest intelligence program in America, focused on issues ranging from arms technology to U.S.-Russia policy intentions, American officials and Russia experts said.

"In fact, the espionage operations designed to steal vital secrets of the United States are as intense today as they have ever been," U.S. Atty. Gen. John Ashcroft said at a news conference Tuesday.

The arrest of Robert Philip Hanssen also underscores a recent and troubling increase in tension between the two governments, analysts said. Suspicions run particularly deep within Russia.

"The Russians now view the United States as the only superpower—and as the only major country that is hostile to its intentions and ambitions," said Dmitri Simes, a 1973 emigre from Russia who is president of the Nixon Center, a nonpartisan foreign policy think tank in Washington.

Part of the tension is due to the different mind-sets of the two new administrations.

Russian Leaders "Much More Nationalistic"

Russia's government is headed by a former KGB general, Vladimir V. Putin, under whom the intelligence and security services in Moscow have far more influence.

"If you look at who's running Russia, it's a much more nationalistic crowd than even two years ago," said Michael McFaul, a Russia expert and senior fellow at the Carnegie Endowment for International Peace in Washington.

"And it's filled with former KGB officers—including the president himself. If you spent your whole life in the KGB, you don't erase that mind-set overnight, or even over a decade," McFaul added.

---

4. Article by Robin Wright from *Los Angeles Times* February 21, 2001. Copyright © *Los Angeles Times*. Reprinted with permission.

In a reflection of Putin's priorities, he has made dozens of trips outside Russia since his election in 2000, including visits to North America. But he has yet to visit the United States, and he does not plan to in the near future.

In the United States, the Bush administration is pushing ahead enthusiastically with development of a national missile defense system, which Russia vehemently opposes.

Moscow warns that the program could lead to abrogation of the Anti-Ballistic Missile Treaty and other disarmament accords negotiated between the United States and Russia over the last half-century.

"It's striking when you look at the kind of issues that dominate relations a decade later," McFaul said. "So many of them are from the same agenda of the Cold War, just with different names: arms control, regional conflicts and European security."

But two recent flash points—the expansion of NATO to include former East Bloc nations and the U.S.-orchestrated bombing of Serbia because of its actions in Kosovo—have contributed to a souring of relations.

"The new wave of suspicions started with the U.S. push for an expansion of NATO," McFaul said. "But the seminal event was Kosovo. Before that, there was a vocal minority of pro-Western liberals [in Russia] who said Russia was integrating into Europe and so NATO's expansion was not harmful. But U.S. actions in Kosovo hurt the prospects of easily resolving differences."

Recurring Spy Scandals a Chronic Irritant

A recent poll reveals the depth of suspicion in Moscow. More than 55% of Russians view the United States as a serious security threat, according to last year's joint survey by the Carnegie Endowment and Harvard University. Only about 1 in 4 said the United States was not a threat.

In contrast, only 8% of Americans view Russia as a top national security concern. China and Iraq were ranked as greater threats by 36% and 15% of Americans, respectively, according to a poll by Penn, Schoen & Berland Associates, a Washington polling group.

There has been a regular stream of spy scandals involving Russia and NATO nations nearly every year since the Cold War's end, providing a chronic irritant to improved relations.

Tensions between Washington and Moscow recently were evident in the case of Edmond D. Pope, an American businessman who was charged with trying to obtain plans for a top-secret Russian torpedo. He was sentenced by a Russian court to 20 years in prison, twice as long as the sentence meted out to Francis Gary Powers in 1962. Pope was pardoned by Putin shortly after the trial and has returned to the United States.

"A Growing Appetite" for Military Tools

In 1999, Russia expelled two American diplomats on grounds of espionage. The United States expelled one Russian diplomat for allegedly monitoring a bug placed inside a State Department conference room. It also charged a Navy code-breaker with selling data to the Russians. Last

> *When it comes to intelligence, the Russians have a long wish list, experts say.*

year, U.S. officials arrested a retired Army officer on charges of spying for Russia for decades.

And when it comes to intelligence, the Russians have a long wish list, experts say.

At the top of the list is military technology. Moscow was stunned by NATO's effectiveness in Yugoslavia and wants to acquire its own arsenal of high-tech weapons, sophisticated electronics and radar detection equipment, Simes said.

"Russia lags significantly behind the United States. And it's concerned about national missile defense, so it has a growing appetite for those things that make America unique in the world," he said.

Political intelligence can be almost as important for the game of diplomatic positioning and long-term goals.

"There's a belief among many in power that you can only trust what you steal, as Russians don't have a tradition of an independent media. For people in epaulets who play a growing role in the Russian decision-making process, it's second nature to look for political intelligence through clandestine collection, even if it's just as easily found on the front pages of the *Los Angeles Times* or the *New York Times*," Simes said.

But just as critical as specific data is intelligence on America's spy program.

"A great deal of what they seek is about intelligence activities. It began during the Soviet period and was carried over by Russia," said Ray Gartoff, a former U.S. intelligence officer and ambassador to Bulgaria who now is a senior fellow at the Brookings Institution, a centrist think tank based in Washington. "That hasn't changed at all, even if there is a greater interest on both sides in seeing whether there are possibilities for resolving differences and having reasonable relations."

Konstantin Preobrazhensky, a former KGB spy in Japan who now works as a political analyst, said Russian officials are no doubt gloating over their success.

"From the corporate point of view, Russian intelligence organs may consider it a big success that they had a spy in such an important position in the USA for so many years," he said. "Even the fact that he was caught can't diminish their pride at this achievement. All agents, no matter how smart and careful . . . get caught eventually."

Despite its ability to cultivate a senior U.S. counterintelligence official, however, Russia has had some difficulty running an espionage operation in the United States, according to Russia experts.

"When you're a failed state like Russia, when you have so many defectors, when you work under the assumption that the CIA and FBI have a lot of assets inside Russian intelligence services, even a greedy American would have to think twice about offering services to Russia because of the danger that it might be short-lived," Simes said.

Spying on China Is Essential to U.S. Security, Analysts Agree[5]

By Keay Davidson
San Francisco Chronicle, April 8, 2001

Far from symbolizing a military intelligence apparatus out of control, U. S. spying on China is essential to track developments in that unsettled part of the world, a diverse array of independent national security analysts agrees.

While some question the Bush administration's handling of the spy-plane fiasco, they insist that spying operations provide vital information to U.S. diplomats who must negotiate the historically and ethnically charged minefield of Asian politics.

"The U.S. intelligence community would be falling down on the job if they avoided paying attention to China," said national security analyst John Pike, often a vigorous critic of the U.S. intelligence and defense establishments. Until recently he was spokesman on space and security issues for the Federation of American Scientists in Washington, D.C., and now is an independent consultant.

"The U.S. continues to have a significant security interest in Asia, and a significant military presence, so the U.S. has an interest in understanding the Asian security environment, which includes understanding China's military," Pike said.

Bay Area physicist Sidney Drell, a veteran adviser to presidents on intelligence issues, said that the more information diplomats have about other countries, the more intelligently they can negotiate occasional crises. That includes, he added, everything from publicly available foreign newspapers to secret foreign documents.

"We get information every which way we can. It's the general principle of a university: The more you know, the wiser you act," said Drell, who recently received the National Distinguished Service Medal from CIA Director George Tenet. Drell is an emeritus professor at the Stanford Linear Accelerator Center (SLAC) in Palo Alto.

The issue for the United States, some analysts stress, isn't so much what China is now.

Rather, the question is: What will China become? For now, no one knows whether Chinese power will continue to grow and eventually dominate all of Asia, or—fractured by economic growing pains and internal dissent—will eventually collapse.

"You hear a lot of alarmist talk about (China)," said Phil Saunders, director of the East Asia Nonproliferation Project at the Monterey Institute of International Studies in Monterey.

"But the reality is that on a global basis, China is nowhere near being a competitor with the United States. . . . They're in a much less powerful position, and their interests are primarily in Asia rather than global."

"Oftentimes, you spy on both your friends and your enemies."— **Phil Saunders, the East Asian Nonproliferation Project**

Saunders added, "What's a more interesting question is: As China's economy and military modernizes, will it be in a position to challenge the U.S. role in East Asia, which is important to the U.S. economically? And as China becomes more powerful, will it threaten Asian security?"

Saunders cited several regional security issues involving China: its territorial claims in the South China Sea, its dispute with Japan over the Senkaku Islands and its problems with Taiwan, which could destabilize the region.

Hence, Saunders said, the need for spies.

"Oftentimes, you spy on both your friends and your enemies," Saunders said. "It's possible for today's friends to become tomorrow's enemies and vice versa. So it's a matter of prudence to be aware of what other countries are up to."

Despite the furor over the spy flights, "this kind of 'passive' intelligence collection—both by us and by them—can actually serve the interests of both countries insofar as it helps to reduce unfounded suspicion and promote stability," said Steve Aftergood, another FAS analyst.

In any case, Saunders noted, "both the United States and China have a long history of spying on each other. (While) it's not clear that Wen Ho Lee was guilty of spying for China, as was alleged, nevertheless it is true that China maintains an active intelligence presence in the United States. . . . A number of Chinese spies have been caught" since the 1980s.

A recent case involved Peter Lee, who passed "a great deal of technical information on to China, including some research on how to detect submarines and some information on how to use lasers to conduct nuclear fusion," Saunders noted. "Lee reached a plea agreement with prosecutors and spent a year in a halfway house."

Said Aftergood: "The intelligence community is plagued by inertia just like any other entrenched bureaucracy. But there are some genuine intelligence concerns connected with China. These include the potential for military conflict over Taiwan, the role of Chinese aid in emerging nuclear programs like that of Pakistan, Chinese arms sales and similar issues.

"More fundamentally, there is a question about the long-term future of the U.S.-China relationship as China actualizes its enormous economic potential and becomes an ever stronger regional power," Aftergood continued. "There are some basic incompatibilities between our two countries, and these are a source of tension.

"I would add: Of all forms of intelligence collection, aerial surveillance from international airspace is among the most benign and nonintrusive. It is quite different from bribing officials or literally stealing secrets."

From Palm-Size Spy Plane[6]

BY STEVEN ASHLEY
MECHANICAL ENGINEERING, FEBRUARY 1998

Keeping aware of situations amid the chaos of combat is one of the most critical but troublesome tasks battlefield commanders must face. Since the airplane was developed, the upper echelons of the armed forces have benefited from ever-greater access to aerial reconnaissance data with which to plan their battles. In recent years, portable satellite data links have started to bring theater-level surveillance information to the lower levels of the military hierarchy nearly in real time. Large-area intelligence assets like spy planes, unmanned drones, and satellites are not always able to provide detailed small-area information to frontline commanders in a timely manner, however. Today's squad leader must still risk troops to scout out what lies over the next hill, beyond the next tree line, or inside the next building.

The Department of Defense is trying to help ground troops at the platoon, company, or brigade level with this crucial task by giving them tiny spy planes, called micro aerial vehicles (MAVs), to search the local terrain. Planners at the Defense Advanced Research Projects Agency (DARPA) envision equipping small combat units with their own "organic" intelligence assets that can locate and monitor possible threats.

Technical evaluations conducted at the Massachusetts Institute of Technology's Lincoln Laboratories in Lexington and the Naval Research Laboratory in Washington, D.C., have concluded that the concept is workable. DARPA is currently launching a three-year, $35 million program to develop MAVs. Negotiations are now being conducted that will lead to Small Business Innovation Research Grants and other types of research and development awards to a range of organizations, including university laboratories, aerospace firms, and small businesses. The agency also plans to select a number of efforts for MAV system development and demonstration.

---

6. Article courtesy of *Mechanical Engineering* magazine Vol. 120/No. 2, February, 1998, pages 74–78; copyright © *Mechanical Engineering* magazine (the American Society of Mechanical Engineers International).

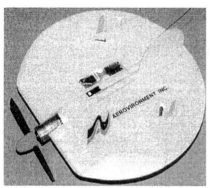

Courtesy of *Mechanical Engineering Magazine*

The Black Widow MAV, developed by AeroVironment Inc.

Several prototype MAV technologies have already shown some promise. Engineers at AeroVironment Inc. in Simi Valley, Calif., have flown a palm-size disk-wing airplane for 16 minutes on lithium battery power. The small Black Widow MAV prototype, which looks like a discus with a propeller, tail, and flaps, awaits completion of its miniaturized computer flight-control, navigation, and communication systems.

Progress is also being made in addressing the need for substantially longer-lasting power sources. IGR Enterprises Inc., a small technology company in Beachwood, Ohio, is developing very lightweight, one-time-use solid-oxide fuel cells that have several times the energy density found in lithium batteries. M-DOT, a technology firm in Phoenix, is working on a diminutive gas-turbine engine that will produce approximately 1.4 pounds of thrust. . . .

Courtesy of *Mechanical Engineering Magazine*

A gas turbine engine, by M-DOT in Phoenix.

These Days, the Cold War Is Getting a Warm Reception[7]

BY PHIL PATTON
NEW YORK TIMES, MAY 2, 2001

"It's the best little museum you can't visit," said Linda McCarthy, who created the Exhibit Center at the C.I.A. in Langley, Va.

For years, the agency's small house museum played host to spies, ex-spies and the odd Hollywood celebrity given special clearance. On occasion, Ms. McCarthy let children from the Make-a-Wish Foundation become spies for a day.

But because the museum is ensconced inside the secretive and secluded C.I.A. headquarters—now named for former President George Bush, the agency's onetime director—the general public cannot come in.

Ms. McCarthy, who left the agency in 1997, is now a consultant to a new espionage museum that regular folks will be able to visit. The International Spy Museum is taking shape not far from the F.B.I. headquarters, a popular spot on the Washington tour circuit, at Eighth and F Streets downtown. The $29 million museum, being developed by the Malrite Company of Cleveland, is scheduled to open next February.

Along with the Cold War Museum being planned for the Washington area by Gary Powers Jr., son of the U-2 pilot shot down over the Soviet Union in 1960, and the increasingly popular National Cryptologic Museum at Fort Meade, Md., a new crop of museums are bringing spies of the 50's and 60's in from the cold.

The Cold War was a virtual war of information, and it was fought by intelligence forces—in the air, on ground and certainly underground. Sunset laws allowing the opening of old files are one reason that museums can now feature Cold War items, said Dennis Barrie, the president of Malrite and the director of the International Spy Museum, which will include a restaurant and spy theme cafe.

"There is tremendous fascination with the whole subject of espionage," Mr. Barrie said, particularly the Cold War, to which about a quarter of the museum's displays will be devoted.

"On the other hand," he added, "for kids, the Cold War is fast becoming ancient history."

Ms. McCarthy said she started the C.I.A. museum largely because "we found that people were coming into the agency with no sense of the history of intelligence gathering. It became an important part of education in the culture."

So popular was Ms. McCarthy's minimuseum at Langley that for years officials discussed ways to open at least part of it to the public. But they could not get around security concerns. Declassification policies have made it possible for some items from Ms. McCarthy's exhibitions, like the camera of a Corona spy satellite from 1960 now in the National Air and Space Museum, to be displayed in public museums.

Along with Ms. McCarthy, Mr. Barrie has recruited consultants to provide artifacts and information for the International Spy Museum. Among them is H. Keith Melton, part of whose 6,000-item

---

"We will have such items as a U-2 airplane, a KH-11 satellite, a fallout shelter and a piece of the wall."—Gary Powers, sponsor of the Cold War Museum

---

espionage collection has been displayed at the Exhibit Center at C.I.A. headquarters, and Antonio Joseph Mendez and his wife, Jonna Hiestand, former C.I.A. officers. Ms. Hiestand was a specialist in spy cameras, what the agency called clandestine imaging. Her husband was chief of disguise and later chief of the graphics and authentication division, the folks who fabricated spy passports. Also helping the museum are a cryptology expert, David Kahn, and a former K.G.B. officer, Oleg Kalugin.

Mr. Barrie said that because so many of the museum's items are tiny—"things that fit into a shoe heel or pocket"—and thus difficult to see, the museum will offer film and videos to compensate. For its part, the C.I.A. has been supportive of the museum but not directly involved. Another feature will be a "spy school," where visitors can learn elements of tradecraft—disguise, for instance. The museum will also have a replica of the famous tunnel dug into East Berlin in the early 60's to tap into East German phone lines.

A piece of the real tunnel—the pipe that lined it—is on display at the Allied Museum in Berlin, housed in the former cinema of the United States military headquarters in southwest Berlin. The Allied Museum also has the Checkpoint Charlie guardhouse, as well as an East German watchtower and a piece of the Berlin Wall.

The wall, of course, is an important symbol of the Cold War, so it also fits into the plans for Gary Powers's Cold War Museum, which still awaits a permanent building. The museum recently became an affiliate of the Smithsonian Institution.

"We will have such items as a U-2 airplane, a KH-11 satellite, a fallout shelter and a piece of the wall," said Mr. Powers, who was born after his father returned from his imprisonment in the Soviet Union. Francis Gary Powers was swapped for the Soviet master spy Rudolph Abel on Feb. 2, 1962. The two men silently passed each other crossing a bridge in Berlin, creating a lasting image of the Cold War.

To raise funds for a permanent facility, some of the Cold War Museum's collection has been touring museums around the world. The traveling exhibition is centered on artifacts belonging to Gary Powers and the U-2, including his flight suit and videotapes of his trial in Moscow.

The museum also sponsors a spy tour of Washington, which includes the suburban house of Aldrich Ames, the C.I.A. officer who for years fed secrets to the Soviets, the mailbox he marked with chalk to request a meeting with his Russian handler, and Pied au Cochons Restaurant in Georgetown, where the Soviet defector Vitaly Yurchenko "redefected" out the back door.

Another stop is the National Cryptologic Museum, outside the National Security Agency in Fort Meade, between Washington and Baltimore, and a memorial park dedicated to the military aviators and intelligence agents who died collecting photo and electronic information on the edges of the Iron Curtain. Some 40 planes were shot down during the Cold War, killing 152 cryptographers.

The National Security Agency, nicknamed No Such Agency because it was more secretive than the C.I.A., scans telephone and digital data sources with sophisticated computers, and is charged with code-breaking. (There are about 13 United States intelligence agencies, by Ms. McCarthy's count.)

The N.S.A.'s headquarters are a set of huge glass and concrete buildings resembling a high technology company. The cryptologic museum, housed in an old motel on the edge of the complex, has a German Enigma code machine from World War II, as well as scrambler phones and computers that were once the most powerful in the world. There is also the "purple monster," a large purple Cray supercomputer that was used for code-breaking as recently as the mid-90's.

For adventurous Cold War buffs, these museums are a fraction of what is out there. Near Green River, Ariz., not far from Tucson, a Titan missile silo complex has been preserved by the Pima Air Museum. The Strategic Air Command Museum outside Omaha shelters bombers and missiles. The bombs carried by the B-47's and B-58's can be seen at the National Atomic Museum—sometimes called the Museum of Doom—at Kirtland Air Force Base, about six miles from the Albuquerque airport. And spy planes are on view at Blackbird Park, not far from Edwards Air Force Base in the Mojave Desert of California. (One of the black birds, a C.I.A. A-12, is on display at the Intrepid Sea-Air-Space Museum in New York.)

Even the former K.G.B. has gotten into the museum business, offering an exhibition of the devices captured from Western spies, in a room of its headquarters in Moscow, open one day each month.

Bibliography

Books

Almond, Gabriel A. *The American People and Foreign Policy*. New York: Praeger, 1960.

Art, Robert J., and Seyom Browns, eds. *U.S. Foreign Policy: The Search for a New Role*. New York: Macmillan, 1993.

Baylis, John, and Robert O'Neill, eds. *Alternative Nuclear Futures: The Role of Nuclear Weapons in the Post–Cold War World*. New York: Oxford University Press, 2000.

Boorstin, Daniel J. *The Genius of American Politics*. Chicago: Phoenix Books, 1953.

Brands, H. W. *What America Owes the World*. New York: Cambridge University Press, 1998.

Callahan, David. *Between Two Worlds*. New York: HarperCollins, 1994.

Clark, Wesley. *Waging Modern War*. New York: Public Affairs, 2001.

Clemens, Clay, ed. *NATO and the Quest for Post–Cold War Security*. London: Macmillan, 1997.

Cox, Michael. *U.S. Foreign Policy after the Cold War*. London: Pinter, 1995.

Cyr, Arthur I. *After the Cold War*. New York: New York University Press, 1997.

Gaines, Post. *Memoirs of a Cold War Son*. Iowa City: University of Iowa Press, 2000.

Gregory, William H. *The Price of Peace: The Future of the Defense Industry and High Technology in a Post–Cold War World*. New York: Lexington Books, 1992.

Gregory, William H. *U.S. Intervention Policy for the Post–Cold War World: New Challenges and New Responses*. New York: Lexington Books, 1993.

Hogan, Michael J., ed. *The End of the Cold War*. New York: Cambridge University Press, 1992.

Johnson, Chalmers. *Blowbuck: The Costs and Consequences of American Empire*. New York: Metropolitan Books, 2000.

Kanter, Arnold, and Linton F. Brooks, eds. *U.S. Intervention Policy for the Post–Cold War World: New Challenges and New Responses*. New York: W.W. Norton, 1994.

Kaplan, Robert D. *The Coming Anarchy: Shattering the Dreams of the Post–Cold War*. New York: Random House, 2000.

Kissinger, Henry. *Does America Need a Foreign Policy?: Toward a Diplomacy for the 21st Century*. New York: Simon & Schuster, 2001.

Mingst, Karen A. *The United Nations in the Post–Cold War Era.* Boulder: Westview Press, 2000.

Owen, John M., IV. *Liberal Peace, Liberal War.* Ithaca: Cornell University Press, 1997.

Thompson, Kenneth W. *Traditions and Values in Politics and Diplomacy.* Baton Rouge: Louisiana State University Press, 1992.

Weiss, Thomas G., and Maryl A. Kessler, eds. *Third World Security in the Post–Cold War Era.* Boulder: Lynne Reinner Publishers, 1991.

White, Donald W. *The American Century.* New Haven: Yale University Press, 1996.

Web Sites on U.S. Foreign Policy

U.S. foreign policy since the Cold War is a very broad topic. For those who wish to find more information online about the subject, this section lists various Web sites that may be of interest. Each one also includes links to other sites that may enrich one's understanding of the topic. Due to the nature of the Internet, the continued existence of a site is never guaranteed, but at the time of this book's publication, all of these Internet addresses were operational.

Columbia International Affairs Online (C.I.A.O.)

www.ciaonet.org
Created by the University of Columbia Press, the C.I.A.O.'s Web site is a detailed source for research about international affairs. The wide breadth of information includes papers from universities, foundation-funded research projects, conferences, and links to journals and books on foreign policy.

Hellenic Foundation for European and Foreign Policy (E.L.I.A.M.E.P.)

www.eliamep.gr
The E.L.I.A.M.E.P. Web site is a forum for the understanding about issues related to European foreign policy, as well as international relations.

Globe Online

www.williams.edu/~globe
Globe Online is a journal designed for students to find information on global issues, including history, politics, science, and technology in a changing world. It centers on scientific and technological challenges of the 21st century.

The United Nations Intellectual History Project

www.unhistory.org
"Ideas are a main driving force in human progress," U.N. Secretary Kofi Annan says in a quote on this Web site's home page. His statement reflects the purpose of this site, to explore the history of the U.N. in the world economy. The U.N.I.H.P. analyzes the evolution of ideas about international economics and social development created under the U.N.

U.S.-China Relations

www.asiasociety.org/specialreports/china.html
This site compiles articles from the press about U.S.-China relations. Created by the Asia Society, a nonprofit educational institution based in New York City, the site has two parts: the first contains articles about documents pertaining to U.S.-China policy, while the second includes background information on the Sino-U.S. Summit of 1998.

Institute for International Economics

www.ie.com/CATALOG/WP/1997/SANCTION/sanctnwp.htm

The Institute for International Economics Web site has a report, written by Gary Clyde Huffbauer, Kimberly Ann Elliot, Tess Cyrus, and Elizabeth Winston, entitled "U.S. Economic Sanctions: Their Impact on Trade, Jobs, and Wages." The report contains links to tables and appendixes pertaining to economics.

Brookings Foreign Policy Studies Program

ww.brook.edu/fp/fp_hp.htm

The Brookings Institute's site contains information, articles, book reviews, and objective analysis about U.S. foreign affairs.

Foreign Policy in Focus

www.foreingpolicy-infocus.org

Foreign Policy in Focus calls itself a "think tank with no walls." Browse by region, topic, product, or media center concerning various scholarly views on world affairs. It contains an extensive array of articles, from drug trafficking to the African AIDS crisis.

The Literature of Intelligence

Intellit.muskingum.edu/intellsite/index.html

With topics ranging from World War I to the post–Cold War world era, *Literature of Intelligence* contains articles, reviews, comments, and essays on intelligence gathering. It includes links to agencies, including the F.B.I. and C.I.A., U.S. spy cases, a description of intelligence, and more.

The Terrorist Research Center

www.terrorism.com

The Terrorist Research Center is an independent think-tank dedicated to the research of terrorism, information warfare, infrastructure protection, and other related issues. The Web site contains current news stories, references, analysis, and more about terrorism, including a selected bibliography.

United States Department of State

www.state.gov

The Department of State Web site covers current events in U.S. foreign policy, press information, and warnings for U.S. citizens traveling abroad. There is also a section on international issues and another highlighting specific countries and regions.

Additional Periodical Articles with Abstracts

More information on U.S. foreign policy since the Cold War can be found in the following articles. Readers who require a more comprehensive selection are advised to consult *Reader's Guide Abstracts* and other H.W. Wilson indexes.

East Asia: Security and Complexity. Marvin C. Ott. *Current History* v.100 pp147–53 April 2001.

Ott's article states that in Southeast Asia, America and China are natural geopolitical rivals. China has recently emerged as a regional great power and an aspiring superpower, something that has been the central development in the East Asian security picture. Over the last decade, while other nations cut military budgets in the post–Cold War environment, China quickly increased its own. Moreover, it is central to three of the region's most dangerous and increasingly dynamic flashpoints: South Korea, Taiwan, and the South China Sea. Since 1941, the U.S. has fought three major wars in Asia, with China an adversary of its forces directly in Korea and indirectly in Indochina. As a product of this history, America has established and maintained a military presence in Asia. With regard to Taiwan and Southeast Asia, U.S. armed forces are a guarantor of security and effectively serve as an obstacle to China's strategic ambitions in the region.

Back to the Bay of Pigs. John Dinges. *The Nation* v.272 pp6–7 April 23, 2001.

Dinges reports on an historic meeting that took place March 22–25, 2001, in Havana, Cuba, in which Americans and Cubans reconstructed and relived the April 17, 1961, Bay of Pigs invasion. For the three days of intensive discussions, the Cuban side consisted of Fidel Castro and 60 of his top military leaders, and the U.S. delegation included five Cuban veterans of the C.I.A.-trained 2506 Brigade, which carried out the invasion, as well as White House advisers Arthur Schlesinger Jr. and Richard Goodwin. The atmosphere was jovial and respectful. At the meeting, Castro and his men could not proclaim more clearly their desire for respect from, if not friendship with, the United States. History and common sense point to concluding a standoff that has outlasted nine U.S. presidents and become an increasingly absurd post–Cold War footnote, but it will not happen as long as the U.S. presidents who control the writing of the final chapter remain caught in a trap of their own making.

China: Searching for a Post–Cold War Formula. Bill Bates and Nicholas Lardy. *Brookings Review* v.18 pp15–18 Fall 2000.

The writers assert that the most complex and critical bilateral relationship that the United States will negotiate in the next ten years is that with the People's Republic of China. Ties between the two countries have been on a downward slope since the mid-1990s and reached a new low in 1999 with the accidental bombing of the Chinese embassy in Belgrade and the snubbing of Premier Zhu Rongji during his visit to Washington. Some positive developments have since occurred, including the completion of bilateral negotiations on China's accession to the W.T.O. The U.S.-Chinese relationship is likely to remain contentious, however, so the new administration should devote a good deal of effort toward integrating China into the international system, fostering cooperative ties with the country, and rebuilding a broader domestic consensus in support of a stable relationship with Beijing.

Bush's Nuclear Revival. William D. Hartung. *The Nation* v.272 pp4–5 March 12, 2001.

Hartung reports that President George W. Bush recently issued a directive instructing the Pentagon to review and restructure the United States' nuclear arsenal. Claiming to revise nuclear policy in an effort to make it more relevant to the post–Cold War world, the Bush administration is espousing an ambitious scheme to deploy a massive missile defense system and develop a new generation of nuclear weapons. Bush's nuclear defense program could cost up to $240 billion over the next two decades. His policy is based on the idea that the United States can and will make its own decisions about the size, composition, and use of its nuclear arsenal without reference to arms control agreements or the views of other nations. This is a disastrous doctrine that increases the likelihood that nuclear weapons will be used again one day, and as such it requires an immediate strong public response.

Why Do We Keep Spying? Massimo Calabresi and Paul Quinn-Judge. *Time* v.157 p40 March 5, 2001.

The writers discuss how the spying game between Russia and the United States is alive and well. In the immediate post–Cold War period, there was a reduction in spying operations by both sides, but as relations cooled in the mid-1990s over N.A.T.O. expansion, U.S. intervention in the Balkans, and Russia's brutal war in Chechnya, both sides returned to their old ways. Russia is seeking strategic data that continue to be important as the two sides start arms control talks and wrangle over a missile shield, information on whether the United States is helping its various enemies, and details about U.S. technology. America's biggest concern is the Russian nuclear arsenal, which is potentially lethal, but U.S. national security officials also focus on terrorism, narcotics trafficking, and other threats.

Completing the Transatlantic Bargain: the United States and European Security. Charles Barry, Sean Kay, and Joshua Spero. *Current History* v.100 pp129–36 March 2001.

The writers argue that a summit is needed to renew the commitment between the United States and Europe by defining a new, more equal balance of influence over transatlantic affairs. In the absence of an obvious threat to Europe, America's influence over the continent's security will be steadily eroded over the coming decade. More equitable sharing of responsibilities indicates not just stronger ties between the North Atlantic Treaty Organization (N.A.T.O.) and the European Union (E.U.), but also lasting vitality for the transatlantic alliance. The United States is gradually moving to accommodate European integration in the fields of security and defense, and drawing N.A.T.O. and the

E.U. together remains the final and most difficult post–Cold War task. Steps that the Bush administration should take to demonstrate its support for the establishment of a European Security and Defense Identity are discussed.

Eyes in the Sky. Simson Garfinkel. *Discover* v.22 pp30–2 January 2001.

According to Garfinkel, in this post–Cold War era, satellite surveillance is no longer the purview of the world's intelligence agencies. SPOT Image in France, Space Imaging of Colorado, and Orbital Imaging Corporation of Virginia have all launched commercial satellites, and the demand for high-resolution satellite imagery is growing exponentially. Intelligence agencies have been quick to take advantage of this new source of information, but orbiting eyes are also beginning to help an eclectic array of citizens do their work more efficiently. Government officials, fishermen, farmers, and real-estate agents are all finding use for the modestly priced images. Moreover, people who never considered the benefits of orbital surveillance could now use the Internet to browse huge collections, pay for the pictures, and download them instantly. A few obstacles must be overcome before the technology becomes ubiquitous, but cheaper images, better coverage, and better use of this resource are just over the horizon.

Humanitarian Intervention: the Lessons Learned. Chantal de Jonge Oudraat. *Current History* v.99 pp419–29 Dec. 2000.

According to Oudraat, the recurring debate in international policy circles on humanitarian intervention has reemerged. Inspired by the Kosovo crisis in 1999 and the Sierra Leone hostage debacle of 2000, this debate centers on the legal, political, and operational dilemmas of coercive actions for humanitarian purposes, and it will only intensify as the world becomes more globalized. In terms of intervention, the effective use of economic sanctions and military force relies on having a clear purpose; accurately assessing the target, leadership, and coalition support; providing adequate resources to ensure effective implementation; and having a suitable strategy. Many post–Cold War interventions that did not meet these standards have failed to have the desired effects.

Do-Goodism Gone Bad. Andrew J. Bacevich. *National Review* v.52 pp30–3 Nov. 20, 2000.

Bacevich explains that the attack on the USS *Cole* occurred as a consequence of American forces assuming a new role. The services must remain ready to engage in wars, but, over the past ten years, their day-to-day responsibilities have come to resemble those of a global military constabulary. The Pentagon's own doctrine now holds that a core mission of the post–Cold War military is to "shape the environment" so as to win friends and influence for America. The *Cole* was sent to Aden not because it was the only port that had fuel available, but because General Anthony Zinni, the recently retired commander in chief of U.S. Central Command and architect of the program of ship visits to Yemen, decided that America needed more engagement in Yemen. America has paid a heavy price for his misguided attempt to curry favor with the Yemeni government.

Next U.S. President Must Lead From Strength. David M. North. *Aviation Week and Space Technology* v.153 p74 Nov. 6, 2000.

North states that both Vice President Al Gore and Texas governor George W. Bush have said what they will do for the military and defense industry if elected U.S. president, but the word leadership is absent from the majority of the prepared statements. The next president must nominate an aggressive and effective individual as Pentagon chief. Numerous senior officers favor Defense Secretary William S. Cohen, but he is frequently viewed as ineffectual. The next secretary needs to be willing and able to lead the transformation of operations that is required to tackle the new security challenges of the post–Cold War age. The future of the proud services, the nation's standing in the world, and ultimately the United States itself will rest on the leadership demonstrated by the next commander-in-chief and his team.

France Perturbed by U.S. Surveillance System.   *Aviation Week and Space Technology* v.153 pp39–40 Nov. 6 2000.

Aviation Week and Space Technology argues that the U.S. National Security Agency's Echelon electronic surveillance system causes profound concerns, may endanger public and individual freedoms, and demands appropriate responses, according to the French parliament's defense committee. The committee has studied available data on the highly classified network and carried out multiple meetings with civil-military security and intelligence experts in France and other European nations. U.S. and British government officials refused repeated requests for further data, however. Such a dismissive reaction on the part of the U.S. administration is generating suspicions, committee members emphasized. In unrelated actions, the alleged post–Cold War reorientation of the National Security Agency's surveillance system to ostensibly intercept phone, fax, and e-mail and conduct economic intelligence is also under investigation by a French prosecutor and the European parliament.

Europe: Rebalancing the U.S.-European Relationship. Ivo H. Daalder. *Brookings Review* v.18 p22 Fall 2000.

Daalder claims that although relations between the United States and Europe are as healthy as they have ever been, the consensus on both sides of the Atlantic seems to be that all is not well. There is a growing feeling that the future does not look very promising, partly because a new disagreement about burden sharing is emerging. Congress has indicated that Europe can no longer take long-term U.S. military and economic engagement for granted, but the European Union's decision to enhance its capacity for independent security action is also worrying for Washington. Any transatlantic security debate involves the question of rebalancing the relationship so that it reflects post–Cold War realities. The writer outlines the challenges that face the United States and Europe in constructing a new relationship.

Foreign Policy in the Age of Primacy. Richard N. Haass. *Brookings Review* v.18 pp2–7 Fall 2000.

Haass reports that the United States is facing several challenges and opportunities from abroad as it enters the second decade of the post–Cold War era. It is likely that American primacy in international relations will continue because no country or group of countries will be able to balance American economic, cultural, and military power for the foreseeable future. The United States will be unable to realize the majority of its ambitions without the support or tolerance of countries such as China, Russia, and Japan, however. As a result, its foreign policy should aim to promote effective multilateralism, which will often call for strong American leadership of informal coalitions and regional groupings. The writer outlines the challenges that will emerge in the areas of missile defense, humanitarian intervention, world trade, regionalism, the Middle East, and foreign policy resources.

M.A.D. No More. Charles Colson. *Christianity Today* v.44 p144 Oct. 2, 2000.

Colson argues that in this post–Cold War age, it is time that America reassessed its defense strategy. The missile strategy known as Mutual Assured Destruction (M.A.D.) worked through the half-century of the Cold War, and neither the Americans nor the Soviets launched a strategic missile and Soviet expansionism was contained. Today's world is dramatically different, however: America is now the sole superpower facing new threats from rogue states, and its strategic defense capability has greatly improved and would be even better if not restricted by the outdated restraints of the 1972 Anti-Ballistic Missile Treaty. Moreover, M.A.D. fails when judged by the criteria of the long influential just-war theory, which holds that the use of force must be in just cause, ordered by competent authority, and used with the right intention. It is therefore time that America adopted a nonaggressive, more just, strategic defense policy.

Apocryphal Now. Gregg Easterbrook. *New Republic* v.223 pp22–7 September 11, 2000.

Easterbrook explains that despite the fact that the American Armed Forces are widely described as crumbling, the country's military is now more powerful relative to its foes than any armed force in history. Some problems do exist, such as the difficulty of recruiting and retaining personnel in a booming economy and the wasteful and underfunded program for weapons procurement. In addition, any attempts by President Clinton to introduce the comprehensive reorganization of the Pentagon that is required to cope with the post–Cold War situation have been prevented by his weak standing with the officer corps. In spite of such difficulties, the United States is the greatest military power in the history of the world and far outpaces its rivals in areas that include nuclear arms, air power, and sea power. The writer analyzes the changes that need to be made in the military's organizational structure.

The Folly of Arms Control. Jonathan Schell. *Foreign Affairs* v.79 pp22–46 September/October 2000.

Schell reports that the post–Cold War period has presented the United States and the world with a choice about the future of nuclear weapons. The Cold War came to an end 10 years ago, but the United States is seeking to stop nuclearproliferation while retaining its own weapons indefinitely, and nuclear restrictions have run into further obstacles such as the tests carried out by

India and Pakistan. It has therefore become obvious that holding on to nuclear arms does not stop other countries from acquiring them but rather goads governments into joining the club. As a result, countries are being faced with a choice between the unrestricted proliferation of nuclear weapons or their complete abolition by international agreement. The writer discusses the crisis of nuclear arms control and outlines the four stages in the development of strategic thinking about nuclear abolition.

Fight Globalization, Theologian Tells Churches. *The Christian Century* v.117 pp858–9 Aug. 30/September 6, 2000.

The article focuses on a leading Christian theologian who has exhorted churches to take tougher action against globalization. Globalization and its negative repercussions, especially on the population of the developing world, have often been censured by churches and related groups in both the industrialized world of Western European and North America and in the developing countries of Africa, Asia, and Latin America. Speaking to 70 delegates attending the executive committee meeting of the World Alliance of Reformed Churches (W.A.R.C.) as it started on July 21 in Bangalore in southern India, W.A.R.C. president Choan-Seng Song referred to globalization as the relentless pursuit of a system of politics virtually wholly dictated by economic domination in this post–Cold War age.

Naming a New Era. *Foreign Policy* pp29–69 Summer 2000.

This article reports that in the absence of icons as memorable as Ronald Reagan and Mikhail Gorbachev, people have understandably been reluctant to imagine a world where such figures have receded into history, and an overwhelming majority of thinkers has stuck with the term post–Cold War era. Nevertheless, 12 years of an epilogue is sufficient, and history, having recorded names such as the Dark Ages and the Enlightenment, is unlikely to remember a prefix. Articles discuss various aspects of the era that has just begun and attempt to give it a name.

The One Percent Solution: Shirking the Cost of World Leadership. Richard N. Gardner. *Foreign Affairs* v.79 pp2–11 July/August 2000.

Gardner states that the federal government's belief that a successful U.S. foreign policy can be executed with barely one percent of the federal budget has serious implications for the promotion of American interests and values. In the post–Cold War era, the Clinton administration and Congress have supported increases in the defense budget to attract and retain quality military personnel but have not considered it necessary to increase funding for the nonmilitary component of national security. Their refusal to view the international affairs budget as part of the national security budget indicates a lack of understanding of the ways in which the United States' domestic welfare is affected by international problems. The next president must rectify the situation because the failure to construct solid international partnerships could ensure expensive military responses in the future. The writer discusses the changes that need to be made in the structuring of the foreign policy budget.

Going Ballistic. Andrew Phillips. *Maclean's* v.113 pp16–18 May 15, 2000.

Phillips explains that the development of a so-called national missile defense (N.M.D.) in the United States is raising questions in Canada about how closely the government should follow its neighbor's lead. The United States is working on a system that it hopes will shield the country from missiles fired by hostile states by knocking them out of the sky with other missiles. The country's post–Cold War defense strategy has many critics, including its allies in Europe and Foreign Affairs minister Lloyd Axworthy, who see it as a dangerous and destabilizing step toward a new global arms race. Officials from the United States have been applying pressure on the Canadian government to back the new scheme or at least to mute its public criticism, which they believe undermines them and encourages European critics. The writer discusses the details of N.M.D. and analyzes how Canada should respond to it.

Let Them Eat Guns. Robert L. Borosage. *Nation* v.270 pp37–8 May 8, 2000.

Borosage asserts that America spends some 17 percent of its total budget on national security and international activities, with the military consuming 95 percent of this total sum. In 2000, the military will receive over half of the entire federal discretionary budget: Spending on international affairs other than the military has been declining steadily since 1980. The starvation of American diplomatic and aid budgets contributes to and mirrors the post–Cold War American default in creating innovative public aid programs and building strong multilateral institutions.

Two Cheers for Clinton's Foreign Policy. Stephen M. Walt. *Foreign Affairs* v.79 pp63–79 March/April 2000.

Walt disputes the general chorus of criticism directed at President Clinton's foreign policy record as unjustified. Clinton has followed a path that has been well suited to an era when there is little for America to gain and lots to lose, and over the two terms he has succeeded in giving the American people the foreign policy they demanded, one that was neither isolationism nor expensive internationalism. According to polls carried out by the Chicago Council on Foreign Relations, Americans believe Clinton's performance on the international stage has been "outstanding," and for this reason the next man in the White House will probably follow a similar line, no matter what happens in the run-up to November. The writer analyzes Clinton's record on foreign events and argues that the outgoing chief executive did quite well considering the post–Cold War circumstances he inherited.

Combat For Sale: the New, Post–Cold War Mercenaries. David Isenberg. *USA Today* (Periodical) v.128 pp12–16 March 2000.

Isenberg alleges that today's mercenaries are highly trained and organized, hierarchically formed into incorporated, registered businesses whose services are offered to governments, large corporations, and government organizations. These new-style mercenaries use innocuous business language, moreover, such as private military companies (P.M.C.s). Often, the members of P.M.C.s are former military soldiers with many years of active service behind them. The new media visibility of mercenaries and the different types of P.M.C.s are examined.

Will the United States Take the Lead? Ramesh Thakur. *The Bulletin of the Atomic Scientists* v.56 p6 January/February 2000.

Thakur states that the United States justifies its own nuclear weapons as vital to national security, but it wants to deny such weapons to anyone else. With the world's most powerful conventional military arsenal, Washington insists on the right to deal with diffuse and ambiguous post–Cold War threats by retaining its ultimate hand, the nuclear stockpile. The lack of a global convention banning the most dangerous weapons of mass destruction is an anomaly and a clear and present danger to the world, and the United States is the sole nation that could successfully lobby for such a convention.

American Power—For What? David Rieff. *Commentary* v.109 pp43–4 January 2000.

Reiff asserts that disputes over America's past hegemony may have little relevance in today's foreign policy debates. From the early days of the Cold War through the Vietnam War to the post–Cold War period, discussions were so bitter and unforgiving that liberals and conservatives still tend, mistakenly, to construe the current U.S. role in international affairs through the prism of those times. At issue is not American hegemony but the attempt to craft a foreign policy that will articulate American interests and values, which is not an easy task. The fact that U.S. foreign policy is subject to so many new pressures is an enormous challenge in itself, creating difficulties with regard to making foreign policy intelligible to America's allies, adversaries, and the general public at home. If such coherence can be attained, much will have been achieved, certainly more than will be achieved by trying to fan the embers of a hegemony that is rapidly in decline.

The 21st-Century Soldier. William Greider. *Rolling Stone* p214 December 16/23 1999.

According to Greider, the U.S. Military Academy is trying to define the mission of the 21st-century soldier. In this post–Cold War era, the soldier lacks any obvious enemy and typically acts as a peacekeeper instead. A more sophisticated type of warrior is needed at this time, which demands a greater focus on the intellectual underpinnings of a soldier, says the academic dean at West Point, Brig. Gen. Fletcher Lamkin. Today's academy is often condemned for training cadets to be smart, flexible, and sensitive to others but failing to give them the will and grit to go into combat. These qualms are extremely unfair to the present generation and neglect the fact that every war—particularly Vietnam and Korea—has been fraught with reluctance to kill, cowardice, and desertion, as well as heroism.

From North Atlantic Neoliberalism to Market Pluralism. Carlos Salinas de Gortari and Roberto M. Unger. *New Perspectives Quarterly* v.16 pp8–9 Winter 1999.

Gortari and Unger report that the current crisis, originating in Asia and affecting nations as diverse as Brazil and Russia, has shown that the global capital market is no savior. Rather, it has become increasingly clear that globalization is mainly to the benefit of a vanguard in the emerging market economies and leaves too many behind as the rear guard. The Asian financial crisis and its aftershocks have shattered the post–Cold War consensus and instilled a broad recognition that the North Atlantic democracies do not have exclusive rights on the market. The concept of market pluralism is superceding the Washington consensus of globalized neoliberalism, and it is ultimately the best solution for all.

Should the Senate Approve the Resolution of Ratification to the Comprehensive Nuclear Test Ban Treaty? Daniel P. Moynihan. *Congressional Digest* v.78 p300+ December 1999.

In a statement first presented during the Senate floor debate of October 8 on the resolution of ratification to the C.T.B.T., the writer argues in favor of ratifying the treaty, asserting that in the post–Cold War era, the United States is the only nation that has the power to shape events all over the world. Moreover, he maintains, as the first nation to develop nuclear power as a weapon, the first to propose ending nuclear tests for further expanding nuclear arsenals, and the first to sign such a treaty, the United States would be sending a ruinous signal if it rejected the C.T.B.T.

Economics as Statecraft. Robert J. Samuelson. *Newsweek* v.134 p58 Nov. 29, 1999.

Samuelson argues that the recent trade agreement with China is a deliberate effort by both the United States and China to influence the world order of the 21st century. The agreement exemplifies post–Cold War geopolitics, where economic arrangements are frequently more important than military alliances. For China, membership of the World Trade Organization would speed up economic modernization by removing protections around inefficient state-owned industries and allow it to realize its destiny as a major world power. America hopes that the deal will ensure that a resurgent China shares—through prosperity, trade, and a growing middle class—an interest in a stable world order, and, eventually, democracy. It is questionable whether these national agendas are competing or complementary, however, and China's risk is greater because the agreement offers few trade concessions.

Index

A-12 spy plane 173
Abel, Rudolph 172
Adams, John Quincy 23–24
Aftergood, Steve 166–167
agricultural bioterrorism 130
AIDS virus 150
Albright, Madeleine K.
    Denis Halliday on 115–116
    military intervention 71–72
    multilateralism vs. unilateralism 15
Al-Gama' Al-Islamiyya (Egyptian
    extremist group) 133
Allende, Salvador 152
alliances 53, 61
Allied Museum 171
Ames, Aldrich 153, 159, 172
Andrew, Christopher 149
Andropov, Yuri 150
Anjoman Islamie 133
Annan, Kofi 71
Anti-Ballistic Missile Treaty 81, 162
Anti-Defamation League of B'nai B'rith
    137
antidrug campaign 48
anti-Semitism 140
Anti-Terrorism and Effective Death Pen-
    alty Act 137
apartheid 118
Apocalypse myth 29–30
Arab-Israeli relations. *See* Middle East
Armey, Dick 15
Armstrong, Anne 143
Ashcroft, John 161
Ashley, Steven 168
Asia, international security 165–167
Assi, Mawzi Mustapha 137
asymmetrical threats/attacks 78, 141
Atlantic Council of the U.S. 23, 40
Augustine, Norman R. 143
Aum Shinrikyo cult 128
autonomy, European definition of 55–56

B-47s 173
B-58s 173
Bacevich, Andrew J. 107

Baker, Rodger 94
balance of power 34, 61, 108–109
Balkan war
    Clinton administration and Bosnia
        22–23
    intervention by external powers 31
    public skepticism about Bosnia 25–
        26
    Serbian aggression 19
Bandow, Doug 18
Barber, Ben 93
Barrie, Dennis 170–171
Bazarte, Byron 137
benefits
    in maintaining air superiority 75–77
    NMD system 83
Berger, Samuel 82
Berlin Wall 171
Betts, Richard 73
bigotry, militia movement and 139–140
big stick diplomacy 71–74
bilateral trade 104–105
Bin Laden, Usama 133–134, 135
Biological and Toxin Weapons Conven-
    tion 129
bioterrorism 128–131, 135–136
birth rates (Europe) 57
Blackbird Park 173
Blair, Tony 115
Boeing Company 76
bombings
    in N.Y.'s black districts 150
    of Serbia 162
    of U.S. overseas facilities 133
    World Trade Center 134
    See also terrorism
Bosnia. *See* Balkan war
botulism 130
Brady Act 139
Brandt, Willy 150
Brilliant Pebbles 85
Brzezinski, Zbigniew 23
budgets. *See* defense budgets
burden-sharing 26
Bush, George H. W. 26, 170
Bush, George W.

189